The PAST is in the PAST so let it PASS:

For Women

The PAST is in the PAST so let it PASS:

For Women

Nadia Atkinson

Be You Nique Publishing

The PAST is in the PAST so let it PASS: For Women
By Nadia Atkinson
Published by Be You Nique Publishing
P.O. Box 95
Matawan, NJ 07747
www.beyoutimes2.com

This book or parts thereof may not be reproduced in any form, stored in a retrieval system, or transmitted in any form by any means—electronic, mechanical, photocopy, recording, or otherwise—without prior written permission of the publisher, except as provided by United States of America copyright law.

Unless otherwise noted, NKJV: Scripture taken from the New King James Version®. Copyright © 1982 by Thomas Nelson, Inc. Used by permission. All rights reserved.

All scripture quotations, unless otherwise indicated, are taken from the Holy Bible, New International Version®, NIV®. Copyright ©1973, 1978, 1984, 2011 by Biblica, Inc.™ Used by permission of Zondervan. All rights reserved worldwide. www.zondervan.com The "NIV" and "New International Version" are trademarks registered in the United States Patent and Trademark Office by Biblica, Inc.™

Scripture taken from the Amplified Bible, Copyright © 1954, 1958, 1962, 1964, 1965, 1987 by The Lockman Foundation. Used by permission.

Scripture quotations are taken from the Holy Bible, New Living Translation, copyright ©1996, 2004, 2007 by Tyndale House Foundation. Used by permission of Tyndale House Publishers, Inc., Carol Stream, IL 60188. All rights reserved.

Cover art work by Janelle Jones
Copyright © 2013 by Nadia Atkinson
All rights reserved.
Printed in the United States of America

DEDICATION

This book is dedicated to my dad, Cecil. Our relationship has blossomed over the past few years and you have encouraged me to be the best me the entire way. Your integrity and unbiased opinion is always appreciated. I admire your strength and willingness to keep pushing forward in tough times. Your love has been perpetual and I thank God for blessing me with you.

I love you.

The Past is in The Past so Let it Pass: For Women

TABLE OF CONTENTS

ACKNOWLEDGEMENTS ix

PREFACE xiii

"My Grace is Sufficient for Thee" 1

Remain Rooted in God 7

Healed by Grace 17

Finding True Love 23

You Are All I Need 29

Finding Love in all the Right Places 35

A Blessing in the Message 43

Living in Faith Every Day 51

Out From Darkness 57

Seek Wisdom in All That You Do 67

God's Everlasting Grace 73

A Shift in the Atmosphere That Brought Inner Peace
.... 79

The Lord Saved Me 87

Loved, Forgiven, and Healed by God to ....
Love, Forgive, and Heal Others in Jesus Name! 95

Joy Comes in the Morning 103

ACKNOWLEDGEMENTS

There are so many people who have been such a blessing to me over the past few years; it is hard to name all of you. Thank you for your constant words of encouragement, prayers, input, and support – without you this book would not be possible. To the two most important people in my life, my parents, Cecil Atkinson and Yvette Correa, I am truly thankful for all the sacrifices you have made over the years. Being parents at a young age was not the easiest thing to do, but I thank you for giving me life because you could have chosen another route. Thank you for your endless support and encouragement when I needed it the most. Mom, thank you for listening when I wanted to vent and yell. I am grateful for our renewed friendship. Your strength and independence made me who I am today. I love you.

To my baby sister, Monika—I am so proud of you. You and I are so much alike that we often bump heads, but at the end of the day, I can always count on you for a wardrobe confirmation and a good laugh. Continue to allow God to be number one in your life and I promise, "All things will work together for your good." I love you sissy.

Gina, Kanisha, Twana, Kay, Lea, and Talisha— you ladies have been such positive forces in my life, especially during this last year. If it weren't for you I am pretty sure this book would have been collecting dust on my hard drive. Thank you for your constant support, words of wisdom, and encouragement. God has truly blessed me with great friends. Thank you.

Dwinel, I want to thank you for being the vessel God used to lead me to Him. You have taught me many great lessons and I thank you for holding my hand during some tough times in my life. May God continue to bless both you and your family.

To all of the women who participated… thank you so very much for sharing your testimonies with me and the world! I will never forget what you have done for me. You have turned my vision into reality. Thank you, thank you, and thank you!

Last but certainly always first, my God, Jehovah. There is no greater love. I cannot express the love that I have for you, yet I know your love is greater. You have healed me, you have given me life, and you have given me hope when I had nothing left. The faith I have in you lets me know you are real. I have never put so much faith in anything, but you reward me with your faithfulness and grace. When I think of all the things you have done for me my entire life, they are indescribable. Thank you for the blood of Jesus, thank you for Your Word, and thank

The Past is in The Past so Let it Pass: For Women

you for placing the gifts that you have placed inside of me. I will continue to listen to Your voice as You guide me toward my destiny. I will forever be yours. I love you forever.

PREFACE

The PAST is in the PAST so let it PASS was a book title God placed in my heart many years ago. I had no idea what I wanted to do for the content of this book but I knew I would find out eventually. A year after I came up with the title, I decided to write about my life and how my past would no longer define me. I wanted to start over again. As I started writing about my life, I suddenly became aware of how many people would and could be hurt by my transparency. I decided I could not do that and did not want to face any negativity associated with the book. I sat on the book for a few more years.

Three short years ago, I dedicated my life to Christ and I started to learn about His works and how He is in the healing business. I decided it was a perfect time to think of writing a book again, but this time I wanted the focus to be on others and not only me. I wanted to tell the story of women who struggled with relatable issues, yet no longer allow their past to define them because Christ doesn't remember their past. As Hebrews 8:12 mentions:

"For I will be merciful to their unrighteousness, and their sins and their lawless deeds I will remember no more."

As I started to develop the idea, God started to guide me toward women who should give their testimonies. I cannot explain how it would happen but I recall walking up to one young lady and saying, "God told me that you're supposed to give your testimony for my book." She did not hesitate and agreed instantly.

I knew that I wanted to ask each woman the same seven questions. I wanted to show that God is no respecter of persons, as Acts 10:34 states, by asking each woman to tell their age and occupation to depict this. After a few short months, I started interviewing the women for their testimonies. I myself was challenged in my personal life and wanted to put the book on hold. I knew I had to press forward and I did, because with God, all things are possible.

My goal for this book is to get as many women to Christ as possible. I know of so many women who are so strong yet feel completely weak. They have no hope, no future, no security, and no love. I know how they feel because I felt that way once, and I know I feel completely renewed now that I have Christ in me. I would never trade it for the world.

I pray this book will allow you to see who God is, how He loves us, and how He is waiting for you to let Him love you. Having that one Person to go to for everything

The Past is in The Past so Let it Pass: For Women

is the best feeling in the world. God has been speaking to you for days, months, and even years, but you won't answer back. Once you are finished with this book, I know your life will be changed, and I know you won't run any longer. Although your situation may seem hard, these women have suffered just the same, and through their stories, you can receive hope in your future with Christ.

"My Grace is Sufficient for Thee"

Age: 27

Department Manager

"Greater love has no one than this, than to lay down one's life for his friends."

John 15:13 NKJV

Tell me what was your life like before Christ?[1]

I was born and raised in a Christian home. I was dedicated to the Lord as an infant as my parents re-dedicated their lives to Christ themselves to raise me to love and know the Lord. I came to accept Christ at the age of 6 after I saw a play similar to "Heavens Gates, Hells Flames." Although I was so young, I realized I was indeed a sinner and sin is what separated me from God, and the only way to God is through his son Jesus.

In my teenage years I fell away from God and got involved in unhealthy relationships with men. I experimented with drugs, got involved with theft, and

---

[1] The first three questions are answered in one large paragraph.

was the best liar you'd ever know. I left home at the age of 18 with my mind set on 'I could make it on my own and I didn't need my parents' guidance.' Nor was I looking to God for anything.

I came to a place in my life where I was being verbally and physically abused in a terrible relationship. I felt literally trapped with no way out and too ashamed to even ask God for help. I was living in a very dark lonely place and I was dead inside. The turning point in my life was when I became pregnant with my first son. I knew then my life had to change. If I was going to raise this child to know Jesus I needed to start showing the 'fruit' in me. God made a way for me to escape the violent relationship I was in and rekindle the broken relationships with my family. I remember one night I could not fall asleep and instead I cried out to God. As soon as I cried, "In the name of Jesus please save me!" I experienced an overwhelming feeling of the Holy Spirit come upon me and I immediately felt peace for the first time in years. I knew then Jesus never left my side and, in fact, just carried me through all of my hardships.

I went back home needing my parents help now more than ever. My parents did not judge me or reject the fact that I was pregnant, but instead welcomed me in with open arms. In fact, my dad could not wait to paint the nursery! The love of Christ was clearly being displayed.

I recommitted my life to Christ and about 6 years have passed since. My life is far from perfect but God has been the supplier for all of my needs and I look to Him for everything. He has blessed me with a loving husband who loves the Lord, three beautiful children with one more on the way, and a career where I am able to share the love of Christ daily. I am forever thankful. I am no longer in a dark, lonely place and dead inside, but alive and a new creation; the old has gone and the new has come.

Revelation 3:20 states that Jesus said, "Look! I've been standing at the door and constantly knocking. If anyone hears my voice and opens the door I will come in and fellowship with him and he with Me." This scripture explains my testimony perfectly. I was afraid to open the door but I am grateful that I finally answered.

What does your salvation mean to you?

Salvation means to me that I have been saved from the penalty of my own sinfulness. I know I am a sinner. I do not deserve eternal life in heaven with God, but He has saved me from the alternative, eternity in hell with Satan. John 3:16, "For God so loved the world that he gave his only begotten son, that whosoever believeth in Him shall not perish but have everlasting life."

If you could save someone by telling them one thing God has done for you in your life, what would it be?

God has shown me unconditional love because God is love. Unlike earthy affection, his love doesn't fluctuate. God didn't care for me more when I've pleased Him nor does He care for me any less when I have failed or sinned. "His love is the same yesterday, today, and tomorrow." His love is the greatest form of love. God's love is sacrificial. He gave His only son to die for my sins so that I may have eternal life and enjoy fellowship with Him while still on earth. That is truly unconditional love!

Tell me why you couldn't imagine your life without God.

Not only could I not imagine my life without God, but more importantly I could not imagine my life without spending my living days giving praise and serving him. God is here for me even before I call on him. He has blessed my family -- time and time again --and He gives me the strength I need to survive.

If you could describe your relationship with God, what would you say about it? How does it help you day to day?

My relationship with God is personal, intimate, and I'm in constant "conversation" with him. He is indeed my heavenly Father and I NEED to call upon him EVERY DAY! I wake up in prayer and sing praises and talk to him throughout the day (on my car rides, at my desk, etc.), praying to him with my children before going to bed, and waking up in the middle of the night to get down on my knees and seek him. My relationship with God helps me to be a better mother and wife. Seeking Him first puts everything else in perspective.

****

I remember as a kid feeling like an orphan. I felt as if I didn't have a great relationship with either parent during my older teenage years. I felt alone, abandoned, and although I acted shy, I desperately was seeking attention. I was always pouring all of my love into my friends. They were my family. When I started dating in high school, men were the closest form of love that I could get because they required more of my time. I always dated a guy who I thought was in it forever. From the beginning I did not want to be that girl who dated someone for two weeks or two months and the relationship was over. I wanted to date as if they were going to be my husband so I chose very wisely or at least I thought so.

Like this young lady, I found myself in a relationship where we argued a lot but we loved one another deeply. It was truly an abusive relationship although we shared many good times together. How many of you know that in order to be in an abusive relationship it doesn't have to be physical? It can also be mental, verbal, and emotional. This relationship was definitely all three. I learned more about myself in that relationship than any other. Since we argued often, I made a mental note to self that I would go into the next relationship, if there was going to be a next, with a little less anger and a little less love and emotion. Sounds crazy but I truly wanted to give less of myself because I was always so easily hurt when we would argue. Two powerful personalities coming together to try to become one was the hardest thing I could've ever attempt to succeed at. That is where Ephesians 5:22 comes into play for sure: "Wives, submit yourselves to your own husbands as you do to the Lord." Although he was not my husband, submission would've done wonders for us. I know that I submitted in some areas, but many areas I was too independent to "allow" someone to control me.

Eventually the relationship ended abruptly and I can honestly say that I never stopped asking God for His guidance in that relationship. I needed a way out and I got one. God was truly by my side all of those years. I started to realize that I found peace in prayer. I realized that there is truly power in prayer. God is always ready to help us in a time of need. He wants the glory and I gave it to Him freely. Let God pull you out of your darkest moments, especially those relationships where you feel that you have no outlet. He will provide a way out as he did for both this young lady and I. Just call on the name of Jesus.

Remain Rooted in God

Age: 26

Student

"Therefore I say to you, do not worry about your life, what you will eat or what you will drink; nor about your body, what you will put on. Is not life more than food and the body more than clothing? Look at the birds of the air, for they neither sow nor reap nor gather into barns; yet your heavenly Father feeds them. Are you not of more value than they? Which of you by worrying can add one cubit to his stature? ..."

Matthew 6:25-34

Tell me what was your life like before Christ?

It's hard to say what my life was like before Christ because being raised in church all my life, I feel like He has always been with me even when I wasn't into Him, so I guess that's the era I'll start from.
Once I moved out on my own at the age of 18, I had a choice whether to go to church or not, I pretty much had "no time for church." I ran the streets with people I had no business being with, smoking, drinking, and pleasing the world. To make a long story short, I got involved with a guy who had a reputation of being very ignorant but that's what the girls in the area liked; and since he "chose" me over the other option he had, I guess to be a

blunt as possible, I thought it was cool. It was the rush of having a boyfriend from the "hood" I guess, everybody wanted him, and I was the good girl with the "bad" guy. Well, that faded really quick, after a year of much unnecessary drama and babysitting a grown man, I became tired of a relationship I knew wasn't going anywhere. I knew it would lead to one road and that was to a destructive lifestyle.

One day he came to my girlfriend's house where I had been eating lunch with friends. I instructed him to come to her house once he found his own transportation. I wasn't ready to leave yet so he said he would be with his "friends" until I was ready to go back to my apartment. About an hour later, my girlfriend, her neighbor, and I all heard a firing off sound but paid it no mind as there was nothing noticeable around us. Moments after that sound, he came frantically around the corner, rushing me to leave. I cannot remember (being that it was over 6 years ago) wondering or thinking at that moment what could have been wrong, I just remember him being in a rush, and me making him wait until I was done helping my girlfriend clean up since we had just finished eating seafood.

When we got back to my house he immediately jumped in the shower, mind you I'm still not thinking anything bad happened. I remembered that I left my crabs at my girlfriend's house and decided to go get them. As I drove past the house where my "bad boy" was hanging out at earlier, I see police, detectives, caution tape, and the remnants of a crime scene. At this point I do remember thinking whatever it is, "HE BETTER NOT HAVE ANYTHING TO DO WITH IT!" Instead of leaving it as a personal thought, when I got back home, I started fussing with him about it. And until this very day I have never heard him say out of his mouth what he did or if he even did it; although he is now incarcerated for murder. As mad as I was when I returned home, he decided to leave which made me even more upset. Once he returned in the morning, I was still on fire and we started fussing all over again, which escalated to the police showing up, him being arrested, and going down to the police station for questioning. All of this happened before he was a suspect in a murder investigation and now I was associated with it all because of the company I kept.

Let's jump to two years later, I was now being charged with tampering with evidence, possession of a handgun, and all of these charges which added up to six in counting. This is all from me leaving with him that night, bringing him back to my place, and last but not least, his sister handing over the gun to officials and telling her story. Who would have ever thought how things can change so quickly? I found myself meeting with a lawyer via phone and face to face for a number of days. I cannot say I turned to God the way I was suppose to, although I know He was on my side because He knew the truth and I never tried to hide anything from Him. I knew I could not hold that kind of burden and still feel until this day that how I handled that situation was meant to be handled in that manner, although it took me through what seemed to be very stressful time of my life.
Day to day, while going through a week-long trial, I was beyond stressed every single day because I was looking at three years of prison if I did not win. Now here is the juicy part: the trial started on a Monday, when Thursday came, I went to church, hurting with worry, not knowing what was going to happen. Then my pastor said, I don't know who I'm talking to but if worry is consuming your

life right now and you're not getting any sleep, come down to the front, and I immediately went to the altar. He said me, "Why?" and in so many words told him, "I'm looking at three years in prison and it's hard to explain but God knows all things." He laid hands on me, and when I went back to court to hear the verdict, I had NO worries at all. I couldn't even believe it although I knew why. All of the other days never felt like that day, and then the verdict was in. As I was sitting in the hallway making my way back to the courtroom, still no worries. My lawyer held my hand as they read out each count/charge NOT GULITY for all except two which required no jail time and only probation. Thank GOD!!! It was all because He knew my heart, intentions, and how I never tried to cover up, hide anything, or manipulate anyone; meanwhile, others were not on my side.

Although a victory had been won, I had a pending case that needed to be dealt with after my trial for being around drug dealers at the wrong place and time, literally. I called out of work one particular day and the DEA decided to raid the house where I was hanging out at. I never really been in trouble, or should I say guilty of any crimes, but I took a plea bargain I didn't understand. Yet, when I went to court for my sentencing, the judge decided to give me 365 days in the county jail, which was only three months with parole. It killed me because I had a three-month old baby. I was getting in trouble for somebody else who was also doing time for dealing drugs. I wasn't even the dealer. I was just associated with him, and I just beat a trail! A case way more serious than this with no jail time, but it was like "really, for this?" Perfect example of guilty by association. In the midst of my hurt, it was like my authority (the judge) has spoken and I have to do this time, be strong, and keep in mind I have God and my family on my side.

I'm proud to say I DO NOT regret going, because I became so humble in two areas, with God and with myself. Spreading the word was the best part, encouraging other inmates, having bible studies, and singing gospel music. I went to church as often as possible and when I heard MY church, Faith Fellowship Ministries (FFM), would be there, I was so proud. It honestly brought me to the place where I am at with my Lord and Savior and still growing in Christ every day.

As far as the "bad boy," I'm no longer in touch with him but I never judged him. No matter what he did or didn't do, I let God be the judge of him. I just hope and pray that God is who he turns to and asks for forgiveness because in my opinion, what he did was a huge mistake. Hopefully the realization will eventually sink in and he will realize that there's nothing out there for you but lessons to be learned if you choose to learn them. He was a lost kid looking for acceptance and unfortunately the streets were all he had outside of me being his temporary girlfriend.

As for the drug dealer, he did his time, came home, and is no longer selling drugs, but instead he has a very successful and promising job that he works very hard for and he is a great father to my son.

This is why I was honored to be part of a Christian book with such a great name "The Past is the Past so Let it Pass." It has done just that and changed my life in Christ tremendously, which will never pass but all that other crap has. Thank God!

What drew you to Christ?

My mom drew me to Christ as a young child but my testimony drew me even closer to Him as an adult.

What made you decide, the day you were saved, that that was the day to dedicate your life to God?

I cannot remember the time I went up to be saved because it was so long ago at FFM but I do remember getting baptized when pregnant with my son in 2010. I was living in Belleville, NJ, attending a church in Jersey City called Tapestry Church. I was really involved at Tapestry and if I'm not mistaken, I went up for a salvation altar call. I really believe I was meant to be there for the period of time that I was there, never forgetting my home church FFM. The pastor of that church helped me get over the fear of dying and all the foolish talk about it, which was a big step for me. This was my first time tapping into my spiritual side openly and seeing other young adults doing the same. One day during fellowship, the Holy Spirit was in that place and when Pastor Anthony called me up to lay hands on somebody else, I was taken aback and thought little old me, but Pastor has made me realize anyone, no matter size, shape, sex or age, CAN lay hands on anyone. I even joined the evangelism team, which was cool. After having my son and moving back to central Jersey, I haven't been back many times, but it's in my heart to visit and have them visit my home church which I love dearly.

What does your salvation mean to you?

Salvation is to be saved. Believing, faith, and no matter how many questions, whatever does not make sense will STILL never be questioned. New life and a new mind; think about it, no matter how many times you fall, get back up because God sent Jesus to do it all for us and as long as you turn to Him, He will never fail you, nor forsake you. I'm so imperfect but my salvation in itself makes all things perfect in Christ.

If you could save someone by telling them one thing God has done for you in your life, what would it be?

He gives me peace. I turn to Him in all things and He's the only one and way of a sound mind and peace in my life. He encourages me to keep going. I would tell someone to PRAY, just turn to God and I promise you'll feel better. Whether you're healing comes right away or not, just wait on Him. No matter how many faults, wrong doing, backsliding, just be honest, make him your best friend, and he'll help you in all areas of your life. You already know what you need help with and cannot do it by yourself. I try to show all my friends and even family that it's OK to let go and let God. He knows just what you need.

Tell me why you couldn't imagine your life without God.

I would absolutely go crazy without the peace He provides. All the impossible He comes up with. Wow. I'm almost speechless in response to this question. So much is going through my mind. I can't even focus. If I depended on this world, I would be in a world of trouble; although we all are already in it, He's my escape! The life after with Him is the bigger picture. We are here to enjoy life and be pleasing to God, and when we can't as "humans," we have to recognize that and pray to be better. If he wasn't in my life I literally do not know where I would be and that's scary. Without the Bible and other Christian books, I would be a wreck.

If you could describe your relationship with God, what would you say about it? How does it help you day to day?

I may be a little repetitive, but my relationship with God is more than I even know. I'm very hard on myself, but have to keep reminding myself God is not a god of remembering everything I did wrong, it's about what I'm doing right and who I'm turning to to make me a better person. I have made Him my best friend because He knows all things, all the secrets of my heart. I am working on myself and my spending time with God because, like my pastor says, we cannot make time for God around our schedule but our schedule has to make time around my time with God.

Praying helps me day to day, just talking to him. When life's aggravations come to attack me, I turn to Him, although the issues don't subside right away. My gospel music helps me day to day, my daily bread, my prayers that avail much, Sunday and midweek services, streamed services from the internet, and just knowing He has my back truly gets me through each day.

****

My early college years were interesting. I did not live on campus but when I was there I would always get hit on by some guy I never seen before. One day one of these guys was in my class and he asked me out on a date after the third week of class. I told him no but I would think about it. Eventually I did and he ended up being a drug dealer. I remember driving in the car with him on our way to dinner and he asked if it was okay to stop by his friend's house. I agreed and I recall him getting back into the car and seeing him put a white substance into the side of the driver's seat. That was when I clammed up and decided this was not the place for me. I asked him to bring me back to my car and he was upset because we hadn't even gone to dinner yet. Foolishly I still went to dinner and still dated this guy for a few months. I never drove in his car ever again; I always met him somewhere, but he was a funny guy and I enjoyed the conversation we had. Finally, he told me that he was out on bail for a federal case. I asked what did he do and he immediately became upset because "I was accusing him of the same crime the feds were accusing him of without even asking if he did it or not." I never talked to him ever again after that night. I did not want to be associated with any criminals, especially with people who place white substances in their cars. I do not know if he was ever sentenced or remained free in the free world, but I pray that all is well.

Just thinking about this testimony that this woman shared, it is amazing how God truly blessed her throughout these tough times. Although she did end up serving time for being associated with someone who did break the law; she always held on to the one she knew for so long, God. Her life could be completely ruined by sitting in a prison cell watching her son grow up through supervised visits and photos. God saved her life in more ways than one. If God is so much more powerful than any government, why wouldn't he save you? God is bigger than any situation that you are going through. God will and can do all things, you can do all things through Christ who strengthens you, allow Him to. This young lady's testimony is a perfect example of how God can turn your life completely around. Just "let go and let God."

Healed by Grace

Age: 28

Qualified Mental Health Professional

"O Lord my God, I cried out to You, And You healed me."

Psalms 30:2 NKJV

Tell me what was your life like before Christ?

As a child, I was raised in the church. I would often go to church under my mother's wishes and never paid attention or valued the words from God but I figured "my presence" in church was enough.

In April 2012, I went to an annual physical check up with no current body pains. I was informed during my appointment that my liver was enlarged. After numerous MRI's and CT scans, what the doctors were seeing was still "unknown and rare." I then went to see a liver specialist who went through all measures to find out what was causing the enlargement. It was discovered that the tumors in my liver came from tumors on the head of my pancreas, which were cancerous tumors. With the doctors knowing this he determined that chemotherapy would not be 100% effective due the amount of tumors that had taken over my liver. The doctors then proposed that I can have a major surgery with chemotherapy to follow.

In September 2012, I had two major surgeries, which was a life changing experience that caused me to lose 30 pounds and no longer like my physical appearance. I had to rebuild my mind, strength, and body. Every pain I felt, every sleepless night, and fear of giving up was guided with a prayer. I repeatedly said in my mind, "I can do all things through Christ who strengthen me."(Philippians 4:13)

Now, almost one year later, I'm tumor-free and didn't need chemotherapy—this is my testimony. In every experience and obstacle that is unexpected one thing that you can control is your faith in God and trust that he will bring you through it. No battle is too big for God.

What drew you to Christ?

My fear of knowing that if I did not go to the doctors in April 2012, my body would have slowly deteriorated and one day I could have randomly lost my life. I know that God brought me to the doctors that day; he had a purpose and plan for me and wanted me to overcome this tragic experience so I could live a long healthy life.

What made you decide, the day you were saved, that that was the day to dedicate your life to God?

When I spoke to my doctor in August 2012 and he diagnosed my tumors as being cancerous, I then realized my lifespan was close to none with the option of major surgery or chemotherapy. I knew once I made the decision to have surgery, which would be most effective for my situation, that I was leaning to God as my surgeon and healer.

What does your salvation mean to you?

It means that life is very precious and don't take every day you're living for granted. Just because you are raised in a church does not mean you truly value and understand God's word. He is a Healer, Protector, and Provider through any situation.

If you could save someone by telling them one thing God has done for you in your life, what would it be?

After being discharged from the hospital my friends and family would often say "don't worry about the bills, rent or anything regarding money." They just reminded me to focus on my health. As much as I wanted to not think about it, I would still wonder how I would survive financially with no income. I spent many days and nights praying asking God for favor and reminding him that I know he will provide for me throughout this healing process. I eventually received disability, all my vacation time from my most recent job, and a friend of mine who was from a previous job heard about my health issues and would send me money every month to pay my cell phone bill. I couldn't help but thank God, knowing he was the Person had made all things possible. Since the day I was unemployed and now a year later, I have paid rent and majority of the important bills while being unemployed with a low monthly income. With this being said, if you remain faithful to God and trust in him, He will make a way out of no way.

Tell me why you couldn't imagine your life without God.

He is the reason I am alive. He built my faith and strength, and continuously reminds me I am His child and I'm blessed.

****

This testimony reminds me of the leper that Jesus healed in Matthew. He asked Jesus, "Lord, if you're willing, make me clean." Jesus responded that He was willing to make him clean and he became clean. She believed that the Lord was going to heal her body and He did. Knowing that four months passed and doctors did not know what was wrong with her speaks volumes because God already knew she was going to be healed. He knew she wasn't going to need chemotherapy. He knew that her income was going to be on hold for over a year, but God! "God shall supply all of my needs according to His riches and glory by Christ Jesus," (Philippians 4:19). He knew that she was going to be taken care of by family and friends. Love thy neighbor! With God all things are possible, all you have to do is believe and He will cure any disease or sickness that your body is suffering from. Don't take ownership of these infirmities. Keep the word "my" out of any sentence associated with illness such as my cancer, my allergies, my ulcers, my high blood pressure, etc. Why take ownership of something you did not ask for? Why take ownership of something that isn't bringing positive attributes to your life? Believe in your healing like the leper, and you too shall be healed. Lift up your head to the heavens and ask God, "Father God, You are Jehovah Rophi, the God who heals, please heal me of this sickness. For I believe in you and I believe that you will heal me, in Jesus name. Amen." It is truly that simple.

Finding True Love

Age: 48

Legal Secretary

"We know how much God loves us because we have felt his love and because we believe him when he tells us that he loves us dearly. God is love, and anyone who lives in love is living with God and God is living in him."

1 John 4:16 TLB

Tell me what was your life like before Christ?

My time was filled with partying and hanging out in all sorts of bars, party lines (like *eharmony.com*, but via phone). I was trying to find the "right" man. I had low self-esteem and did not like who I was. This opened doors to interests in pornographic readings and novels, new age resources like horoscope, and horror movies. I was obsessed with this lifestyle.

What made you decide, the day you were saved, that that was the day to dedicate your life to God?

I grew up in a Christian home where we went to church on a regular basis. However, my parents were not knowledgeable about the things of God or the Bible. So we were taught very minimal about God. On the other hand, when I was around 9 or 10, I attended a vacation Bible class at this church. The instructor taught on Psalms 23. I'm not sure if it was a salvation experience, but I received an understanding that God was my shepherd and that He cared for me. I was so alive! I kept this experience to myself. Over time, the experience of that "moment" left me.

Fast forward years later, I was in my late twenties early thirties, a girlfriend who I was very close to in high school called me from the same number my parents had since high school! I could not believe it! The telephone number was very old but she kept it. We talked a bit and she asked me about going to church with her. I declined. At this time I was not attending anything church related! This went on for a while, her calling me, asking me to attend church with her, me declining and having "things" to do. She never gave up. Finally, I got tired of her asking and I told her yes. She attended Faith Fellowship Ministries at the time.

When I walked in, I was very uncomfortable to say the least. People were praising God, etc. I did not come back for a while because I thought those people were crazy! After some time went by, my high school girlfriend calls again to go to church with her. I went to get her off my back. That day, Pastor Demola at the end of teaching asked us to repeat the salvation prayer from our seat. BANG! I was changed! Instantly! Words cannot explain it. I literally went from darkness to light. I was completely delivered and set free!

What does your salvation mean to you?

My salvation is very precious to me. This is a gift that opened my eyes to the world around me and this gift is available to and for everyone.

If you could save someone by telling them one thing God has done for you in your life, what would it be?

The one thing I would tell someone is that He let me see how valuable I was to Him. Through teaching and reading the Word, I had to realize it was not what I thought about myself or what others thought of me; it's what HE thought about me. This understanding of being valued set me free. God saw *me* as valuable. Wow.

Tell me why you couldn't imagine your life without God.

Life without God will be an endless pursuit of trying to find meaning and purpose in life. I tried to find meaning in life via meeting men on party lines, trying to find the perfect "ONE." I said to myself, "Maybe I will find the perfect 'ONE' to marry and we have a great life." So I thought. Many of them were broken individuals who had hang-ups, too. Broken + Broken = Misery. My life without God will be meaningless, hopeless, and bleak. My life with God is exciting and complete.

If you could describe your relationship with God what would you say about it? How does it help you day to day?

My relationship with God is exciting and it is always learning about who I am in Him! His Word is my life. I spend time in the Word so I can know His ways and thoughts. I "hear" Him in the reading of the Word. Day by day, I am always conscious of His presence just by saying the name of Jesus or singing a melody. My relationship with God is built on prayer, listening, reading the Word, and doing what pleases Him.

****

I recall being like this young lady. I wanted to feel loved and I sought out love in all the wrong places: the club, in alcohol, in marijuana, in men, friends, in horoscopes, and I couldn't seem to find what I was looking for in any of these areas. For years, I went from relationship to relationship praying that "this guy would be the one." I knew my worth and I knew what I could bring to the relationship, but I was tired of feeling empty. I was tired of allowing my emotions to get the best of me. I was tired of searching for men who matched my zodiac compatibility. I was tired of feeling like no one loved me.

I felt alone and depressed. I could not find what I was looking for anywhere. I thought I found it in a guy I dated, but he let me down too. After that, I knew it was time to leave all of the drugs and clubs in the past and move forward toward a brighter future. Then I discovered God.

It was as if He had never left my side. I always prayed to God since I was a teen so I was not sure if God heard my prayers or not because of my hiccups, but He did. I recall sitting in church for the first time as an adult and feeling awkward. I felt like I did not belong there. I felt that everyone was staring at me. I felt uncomfortable because of all the wrong I did in the past. I felt this way for weeks, even months, then finally I had a sense of freedom…breakthrough.

I want you to feel that same way. Many of us as women can't even imagine what freedom feels like with work, children, husbands, bosses, businesses, and maintaining the home! The thought of being free sounds like a vacation that lasts longer than seven days, but you can't quite envision it because it seems impossible. Allow Christ to work in your life, "submit to Him and He will make your paths straight." (Proverbs 3:6) I promise you that vacation that is long overdue could be a few words away.

You Are All I Need

Age: 54

Homemaker, Advocate, Travel Agent, Counselor, Teacher

"When I walk into the thick of trouble,
keep me alive in the angry turmoil.
With one hand
strike my foes,
With your other hand
save me.
Finish what you started in me, GOD.
Your love is eternal—don't quit on me now"

Psalms 138:7-8

Tell me what was your life like before Christ?

My life before Christ was full of confusion with no sense of purpose. My role in a family of nine siblings was the elder daughter who didn't have much of a childhood. I had to assume the role of caretaker, which meant to clean, be the babysitter, feed my siblings, and help with homework at a young age. We had to go to church, where we learned the scripture but no personal relationship with Jesus. When I became a teen I rebelled, but pretty much still did the chores to gain my freedom outside to escape the house that was not a home. My Mom had many relationships after my Dad and her split. There were many fights, drugs, people in and out of jail, homelessness, and living with relatives. Our family was all over the place. There was so much unstableness and confusion. Our home was unstable and full of confusion.

What drew you to Christ?

My Mom moved to Staten Island, NY, at the last minute because one of my brothers had a death threat. Due to the last-minute notification (and I didn't want to leave my friends), I asked my Mom if I could stay with an aunt who was in the area. I was kicked out of my aunt's home, she was an alcoholic and I was hanging out too much. When I reached my mom's home with my two pieces of Puerto Rican luggage (two brown shopping bags), my Mom said I was just praying for you. I said "Yea, OK." A few days later, I was asleep in my room, the moonlight was shining very bright in my room, and I heard someone call my name three times at about 3:00 am. Each time I walked into the living room, everything was dark, no one was there, and I walked back to my room. The last time I went back to my room, I fell to my knees and started to weep. I asked Jesus to come into my life and I was able to sleep like a baby. The next day I reluctantly told my Mom I had accepted Jesus as my Savior.

What made you decide, the day you were saved, that that was the day to dedicate your life to God?

The Spirit of God was revealed in my heart.

What does your salvation mean to you?

Salvation means to be saved and delivered from myself and this world. He chose me!! David wrote in the Psalms, "What is man? That thou art mindful of him."

If you could save someone by telling them one thing God has done for you in your life, what would it be?

I would tell them of God's unfailing and unconditional love, able to restore and renew what the enemy tried to destroy. There were many hurts in my life: dysfunctional family, bad relationships, and people constantly putting me down. God has given everything back far more than I could have ever asked or thought. God truly gives you "double for your trouble."

Tell me why you couldn't imagine your life without God.

One day I was in the hospital ready to check out of this Earth, my pupils were pin point from going through a bad relationship. But God was not finished with me yet. Even though I was giving up, God had a different plan. His ways are not our ways. He is my Guide, my Best Friend, my All in All. This is all motivated by His love for me. He knows everything about me. He has my best interest in mind; He has no hidden agendas!! I love my God!

If you could describe your relationship with God, what would you say about it? How does it help you day to day?

My relationship with God is a moment-by-moment, day-by-day relationship. He is all I need. He is my God; there is no one else!! God is first, my Husband is second, my family is third, and then my church family! That is the only order which life should be lived. God is above all.

****

Many of us women have been trained at a young age to support ourselves and take care of the family. Hearing what this woman's life was before Christ may sound a lot like your story; it may have given you goose bumps just reading it because it hit home.

Carrying the weight of the world on your shoulders doesn't start when you're an adult; it starts at a young age. Many of you did not have the home with two parents and the white picket fence. Many of you did struggle with your parents. Unfortunately, your parents may have grown up while you were growing up because they were so young. They learned by trial and error. Now as adults, we can't help but to look back on our lives and wish that they were different.

But God! He will shine light on your darkness. You may be called in the middle of the night to pray and give your life over to Christ as this woman experienced. You may be called in the middle of a work day to give your life over to Christ. You may be called to Jesus in a church service. You never know when Jesus will decide to whisper in your ear asking, "When will you let me help you?" You will never know. Stop fighting it and run toward Him. You have run in the opposite direction long enough. He has spoken to you numerous times before, over and over and over again. Your family keeps telling you to give your life to God. When will you stop fighting the battles on your own and allow God to do them for you? For Romans 12:19 states, "Beloved, do not avenge yourselves, but *rather* give place to wrath; for it is written, 'Vengeance *is* Mine, I will repay,' says the Lord." Let today be the day you give your all to God. He is waiting.

Finding Love in all the Right Places

Age: 56

Executive Director of

Strengthening Women Beyond Abuse

"He brought me up also out of an horrible pit, out of the miry clay, and set my feet upon a rock, and established my goings."

Psalms 40:2 KJV

What was your life like before Christ?

Before Christ, I came from an orphanage in Farmingdale, NJ. I lived there for fourteen years and had the best time of my life. I went to school, church, lived there full-time, and it was the best childhood a girl could ask for. Then the State of New Jersey decided that mothers could take better care of their children so I was turned over to my mother. That is where I learned about lying, sexual abuse, domestic violence, child abuse, and being poor. My stepfather sexually abused me the very first night I came to live with my mother. My mother could no longer support me so she sold me to an African American male who was 35 years old.

I was locked in my apartment for 22 years until one night I said to the Lord if He didn't get me out of there that I was going to kill myself. The next morning, I noticed that the door was cracked open and I ran and never looked back. I was a Catholic, practiced Santeria, a Methodist, and a Christian. I didn't care about anyone, but I cared about marijuana, sex, lying, and money. As long as I could get sex for money with no attachments or love, then smoking marijuana and being depressed was OK.

After a couple of years, I became a cutter and slept in closets because of severe depression. I started to go to a church and started to hear the Word and joined the choir. I continued to smoke marijuana and have sex with men of the church. Eventually, one of the men told the pastor and I was told to sit in the back on the mourner's bench. I sat on the mourner's bench for a year until the depression got worse and I tried to commit suicide. Soon after, I met a woman named Dina and she took me to Rev. Deborah Cooper, and the Holy Spirit changed my life. I used to say to Rev. Cooper that "this was my story and no one was ever going to take it away from me." I now am happy to give it away. I continued to go to the hospital because the depression was getting stronger the more I learned about Christ. Just because you become a Christian that does not mean that the battle is over, you have to continue to fight for your life.

What drew you to Christ?

I remember a Pastor from another church asking if anyone wanted to give their life to Christ. All of a sudden, a deacon came to me and said, "Don't you want to give your life to Christ?" and I said "no!" She said, "Yes, you do!" and pushed me up to the altar. I don't remember repeating any words. I was sent to the bottom floor and asked to wait for a deacon, but no one ever came so I left. My friend Dina introduced me to Faith Fellowship in Sayreville, NJ, and I started to learn the true Word of God. I was reading a book called "God Chasers" and that is where I got saved in my living room, alone with Christ.

What made you decide, the day you were saved, that that was the day to dedicate your life to God?

My tears made it clear that I needed to believe that God truly loved me. His love touched my heart in a place I never felt before. Rev. Cooper reminded me of God's love for her and how I could also receive that same love even with all the anger, pain, and sins. Then I read a book called, "Hinds Feet on High Places" by Hannah Hurnard. What a Blessing it was.

What does your salvation mean to you?

Salvation means trusting in God. You can't touch Him, see Him, or smell Him, but you know that you know that He is real. When He can speak to me, it makes me cry because He takes time to encourage and guide me through the day. God is so special. Salvation means having the opportunity to start life over with a clean plate.

It also means newness, and God helps you create a right spirit in you.

If you could save someone by telling them one thing God has done for you in your life, what would it be?

It would be to trust Him. My trust was in man. He is the only person that I know that I can trust. When I learned about faith – what a revelation! I was always lying because I didn't want anyone to know what I was doing and didn't want them to know that I was using drugs or cutting my skin so that I could feel pain. When I was told that if I have faith as small as a mustard seed that God would help me to heal my mind and my pain. I say mind because I didn't want to give up my story and my pain. I am healed and better for it because God took the scales off my eyes and I can clearly see now. It is not an overnight process, but eventually you will get there.

Tell me why you couldn't imagine your life without God.

Listen, I said I am either going to go hard for Christ, or go back to cutting, drugs, and sex. I have been homeless and I always called on Christ and he took me out of the miry clay. Think about clay, it is dirty and sticky, and that is a very uncomfortable feeling. It was important for me to be clean. I like the cleanliness of Christ's love. I still have my struggles, but in the long run I'd rather have Jesus than nothing at all.

If you could describe your relationship with God, what would you say about it? How does it help you day to day?

I wake some mornings crying for that little girl that was never allowed to grow up to be herself, but I know my process has been painful, but I BELONG TO CHRIST. My relationship is sweet. He wakes me up just to tell me He loves me. He supplies all of my needs and takes away my sorrows. Many people don't understand, but when my father died this year, I realized that I had a love that made me understand that I was his daughter. There is nothing like the love of your father and God.

****

Although this young lady had many obstacles from her early childhood years into her adult years, the Lord had His hand on her life. He slowly guided her back to Him. He had the door cracked just enough for her to escape from her past. He used her friend Dina to bring her to His house for counseling and to know His love. God is for you and not against you. In the midst of cloudiness and confusion, there He is waiting to see if you'll call on Him for help, waiting to see if you will recognize Him in the doorway to freedom. Just call on the name of Jesus, He will save you!

I recall a time when I could remember writing poetry for hours. In class, at home, in my room, it didn't matter where I was; I had something to say, and most of the time it was dark. Poems filled with anger, death, and struggle, all at the tender age of 12. I too wanted to commit suicide. I often would think about the easiest way to take my life without feeling any pain. I recall writing a poem asking, "What would you do if you found me at the bottom of a lake?" It wasn't until I started reading the Bible that I realized my life was just as important as the people in the Bible. God saved me! Not once, not twice, but on numerous occasions. I couldn't tell you how many times, but I am thankful that I listened to His voice. The thought of me taking my own life at 12 and not going through some of the trials and accomplishing the goals that I have set for myself is mind-boggling.

I think about the account in Job 1 when Satan had a conversation with God, and the decision was made to tempt Job. I read this account and think of my life as a child. Satan was trying to tempt me. He almost won, but if it weren't for those trials, if it weren't for those valleys, if it weren't for God protecting me, I would not be able to bless the Kingdom of God with this book today. Job 1:6-12 reads:

> *"⁶ Now there was a day when the sons of God came to present themselves before the LORD, and Satan also came among them. ⁷ And the LORD said to Satan, "From where do you come?"*
>
> *So Satan answered the LORD and said, "From going to and fro on the earth, and from walking back and forth on it."*

⁸ Then the LORD said to Satan, "Have you considered My servant Job, that there is none like him on the earth, a blameless and upright man, one who fears God and shuns evil?"

⁹ So Satan answered the LORD and said, "Does Job fear God for nothing? ¹⁰ Have You not made a hedge around him, around his household, and around all that he has on every side? You have blessed the work of his hands, and his possessions have increased in the land. ¹¹ But now, stretch out Your hand and touch all that he has, and he will surely curse You to Your face!"

¹² And the LORD said to Satan, "Behold, all that he has is in your power; only do not lay a hand on his person."

So Satan went out from the presence of the LORD."

This woman's description of the miry clay and her yearning to be clean and free in Jesus is so symbolic and beautiful. God wants the same for all of us. I know that I wanted the same and I know you do too. Just call on the name of Jesus. Do not give credit to Satan and his demons, for they know us better than most people because they have watched us grow from children to adults; however, Satan has already been defeated. He is trying to bring as many people down with him before his time is up. Only a fool gets kicked out of heaven. Continue to stay optimistic and look for the crack in the door. Your breakthrough is coming. It came for this woman, and it will surely come for you.

A Blessing in the Message

Age: 28

ER Clerical Representative

"Now faith is the substance of things hoped for, the evidence of things not seen."

Hebrews 11:1

Tell me what was your life like before Christ?

My life before Christ was not that exciting. You know growing up as a PK (Preachers Kid) I was always going to church and never really could do anything. So for me, I felt as though Christ was good but I thought that the world was everything to me. I wanted to do what I wanted to do. Everything I did would always get me into trouble. I knew the right thing but I wanted to do what I wanted to do. I was never a troublemaker. I was sneaky and rebellious. Life seemed as though nothing was turning in my favor. As I got older, I began to see what Christ was all about and started to get more involved in church. When I did attend church, there was always a message that would convict me. I would go up for prayer and receive Christ and say that I am saved. As soon as I would leave, the enemy was always waiting to tempt me. My life was going through its ups and downs. My family and I didn't always see eye to eye; my siblings and I were always going against one another. I was always feeling like no one cared for me. There was something I was missing. I was empty. Then, I met Jesus Christ.

What drew you to Christ?

What drew me to Christ was the first year I went to *MegaFest* in Atlanta, GA (*MegaFest* is a weekend that includes a host of empowerment sessions, inspiration, prayer, and entertainment.) I will never forget that day. I was very excited about going with family and friends. I got saved at a young age but I backslid (When a Christian turns from God to pursue one's own desires). I repented to God and asked for forgiveness. Being at *MegaFest* was the best year ever. I remember seeing Kirk Franklin, Shirley Caesar, Tonex, Bishop T.D. Jakes, and more. It was that night that Tonex was performing and ministering his song "Lord Make Me Over." As he began singing and ministering the song, tears began to roll down my face; I began to cry out and ask the Lord for forgiveness. That's when I decided that I will give my life to Christ. I told the Lord that I surrender to him. That song still ministers to me and I still continue to ask the Lord to "make me over." We all need to ask the Lord to make us over sometimes. As I recall walking back to the van, I was still full with the Holy Spirit. The Spirit was so heavy that we had a parking lot ministry, as the adults would call it (We continued it in the parking lot). God is so AMAZING. Even as I am sitting here saying this I am getting overwhelmed. When I got back home I threw away every R&B and rap CD I had owned. I started trying to live a life pleasing to God. That's one of the reasons that drew me to Christ.

What made you decide, the day you were saved, that that was the day to dedicate your life to God?

Once again, the song "Lord Make Me Over" is a very powerful song. I would always hear the preachers and my parents saying, "You need to get saved!" or "You need to get your life right before Christ returns!" I would always hear that playing in the back of my mind. I always had a relationship with Christ but it wasn't as strong as it is today. I can remember being in church on New Year's Eve and my father had just finished speaking. He began to minister and speak over other's lives (prophesy). On December 31, 2011, I rededicated my life back to Christ and I've been going strong ever since. I told God that I was ready to do His will. God began dealing with me on some things and blessing me with others like my first youth conference to run. It was a blessing. I am a soldier on the battlefield for the Lord!!

What does your salvation mean to you?

My salvation means everything to me. Being delivered from sin and sickness is a blessing. Jesus died on the cross for my sins. How can I not be thankful for my salvation? Every time I pray, I thank God for salvation. If it had not been for the Lord who was on my side, where would I be? Just imagine being free from everything. That alone is SALVATION. Thank you Lord!!

If you could save someone by telling them one thing God has done for you in your life, what would it be?

If I could save somebody by telling them one thing God has done for me in my life it would be when God blessed me with my current job. There are so many things I could say that can save someone. This particular situation was special because I had lost my job in December 2011. I had been looking for a job for months and months. It seemed as though no one was hiring, or you had to have three-plus years of experience. I went to school to be a Medical Assistant and it seemed my work experience wasn't enough. So I began to pray and talk to God.

Then one day I got a call from my sister in-law telling me that her friend's job was hiring, so I said OK, I will give it a shot. The next day I called the place, which was a very well-known public health care provider, and the position was for a Customer Service Representative. I would handle incoming calls to set up appointments for abortions; I decided to set up an interview. After I got off the phone, I began to sit and think about the job. Being connected to God, I knew I couldn't handle women calling in to schedule an appointment to abort their babies. I don't agree with the idea of abortions. I just couldn't shake the feeling. I immediately began to pray and talk to God and ask him for clarity and guidance. I asked God to show me if this job was for me. For an entire week, I would wake up with a headache and go to sleep with a headache, praying and crying. It was driving me up the wall. On a Tuesday night after our family gathering (Bible Study), I was talking to my First Lady (Pastor's wife) sharing with her what I had been going through for the past few days. She started telling me a similar story that I could relate to. That's when I realized that this job wasn't for me.

I returned home that night and received a text message about 10 pm that evening from my previous coworker asking if her sister could call me, I agreed. I get the call from her sister telling me about a position at the hospital. I've always wanted to work at the hospital. She told me to go to the hospital's website, fill out an application, and notify her when I finished the application. I completed the application that very night. The next morning I had informed her that it was completed and in two days I got a call from the director of the Emergency Department! Just seven short days later, I was hired!!!! You can't tell me God isn't good. I absolutely love my job!!!! I realized that if I was not faithful to God and I was not happy for others when God blessed them, I would have not been blessed with my job. I would always hear people say be happy for others and celebrate with them. Everything my friends or family members were blessed with, I would tell them, "I'm happy for you and I know my blessing is on the way." If we remain faithful to God, He will remain faithful to us. I leave with this: "But seek he first the kingdom of God and his righteousness; and all these things shall be added unto you" (Matthew 6:33).

Tell me why you couldn't imagine your life without God.

I've been blessed with so much. I couldn't imagine what my life would be without God. God is the center of my joy. Without God, I am nothing. If I don't have God I might as well be dead. God is the air I breathe. God is The Alpha and The Omega. You know the saying, "God is mmm good!!" Jason Nelson summed it all up. I'm nothing without You!!

If you could describe your relationship with God, what would you say about it? How does it help you day to day?

My relationship with Christ is GREAT. God is the great I Am. In order for me to stay connected with God I pray. Prayer is how I communicate and feed my Spirit with His Word. Some days God and I have humorous days. When something happens, all I could do is say, "God you are funny." To get through my day-to-day life, I must pray. Prayer is the number one key for me to stay connected to God. If I don't pray, I feel off and my day and/or week do not go the way I want it to go. I find myself sometimes asking the Lord to forgive me if I forgot to pray when I was out and about doing my day-to-day duties. I immediately stop what I am doing and go into prayer. Having faith goes along with my day-to-day life and having my relationship with God is indescribable. God is AWESOME!!

****

This testimony touches my heart deeply because I was faced with the decision of becoming a mother or aborting my baby in my early twenties. The man I was with for a few years never told me that he wanted to keep the baby until after the abortion was completed. It was ultimately my decision. I knew that abortion was wrong because I grew up in a religious yet divided household, so I knew that I would have to hide this forever. I have from most until just now. I would go to my grave with this as many women do, have, and will. When I was in the room waiting to receive the anesthesia, all I kept thinking about was all the things I would not be able to offer this child if I were to have him or her. I was young and could barely support myself, yet I was supposed to do this on my own. I knew that my boyfriend at the time would have never left my side if we were to bring a baby into the world, but I just could not do it. Today, this is the only thing that I regret. That is why I cherish the verse Jeremiah 1:5 so much. I convicted myself for years. I put myself and boyfriend through the craziest emotional roller coaster for nine months. We weren't pregnant, but we would visit *Barnes and Noble* to view pregnancy books and view the babies' progress on our cell phones as if we were. It was completely unhealthy and eventually I grew to hate him. I know it was my decision, but I wished he stepped up to the plate and told me not to abort the baby. It was indeed someone who God appointed me to carry and I didn't cherish what He gave me. I know that I will be blessed with a little one when God says it is my time, but for now, all I want to do is encourage someone. God will provide for you financially, mentally, and emotionally. Have that baby; do not let anyone convince you, including yourself, to abort your baby. There are so many people that I know whose parents were supposed to abort them and they all are successful. ALL—OF—THEM!

"Before I formed you in the womb I knew [and] approved of you [as My chosen instrument], and before you were born I separated and set you apart, consecrating you; [and] I appointed you as a prophet to the nations."

(Jeremiah 1:5)

I have no idea as to why this is on my heart to express. I knew I was going to my grave with this. I tried to talk myself out of writing this, but I know someone needed to read this. I do not care if it is one person, I know that someone will give birth to a scholar who will glorify God and dedicate His life to God's Kingdom. Just put your faith in God, He will not let you down. God will never go back on His Word. He is perfect.

Living in Faith Every Day

Age: 32

Songwriter

> "…For I will surely deliver you, and you shall not fall by the sword; but your life shall be as a prize to you, because you have put your trust in Me," says the LORD.' "

Jeremiah 39:18 NKJV

Tell me what was your life like before Christ?

Before Christ, I lived a life with no direction. I believed that the only person that guided my life was me and those around me. I hung around people who lived a negative lifestyle, and even had those people around my child. I lived a promiscuous and dangerous lifestyle, and at the time, it was fun. I didn't do drugs, but I allowed myself to be around them and allowed them in my home. I was 19 years old with my own apartment thinking I could do whatever I wanted, never thinking about consequences, or the danger I was putting my daughter in.

What drew you to Christ?

There had come a time when I had hit rock bottom. I was about to be evicted from my home and I needed help and none of the so-called friends that I had around me every day could help me, nor could any of my family members. Everyone had an excuse as to why they couldn't help me. It was then that I realized that I could only depend on Christ. I don't remember exactly how it was resolved, but it was from then on I decided I would never put my faith in man again.

What made you decide, the day you were saved, that that was the day to dedicate your life to God?

I became saved when I was young. I attended church on a regular basis due to my mother and stepfather making it a requirement. I said the words and I prayed the prayer, but I never really took it seriously. In my mid-twenties, I was dating a gangbanger who I thought was a great guy but had the bad boy thing going for him that I loved. I never thought that I would ever see that bad boy side of him. One day I decided I was going to check his voicemail on his cell phone, and I did. It was easy because men never use passwords that can't be guessed. Well I told him I did, and I don't know what he thought I heard, but there was something on there that he didn't want me to hear. I confronted him about a girl's message that was on there, but he didn't care about her message, he was just angry that I checked his messages. He threatened to kill me, and knowing that he was capable of doing just that, I was scared. He knew where I lived with my daughter and he knew where my family lived. I left my home for about a week. I was staying at my best friend's house who just so happened to live across the street from a church.

The following Sunday I attended one of the services at that church. I prayed and I cried like I had never prayed and cried before. I promised God that I would change my life if my life was spared in this situation. I dedicated my life to Christ that day and I meant it with my whole heart. When the service was over, I felt a weight lifted off me, but I wasn't going home just yet. I went back to my friend's house and she told me that while I was gone a lady knocked on her door to get help because she was having car trouble. Now my friend lived in an apartment complex, so the lady could have knocked on 10 others doors that were around my friend's house. My friend welcomed the lady in to make a phone call. Before the lady left, she told my friend I don't know what's going on, but know everything is going to be fine, and then she left. Till this day, my friend has never seen the lady ever again. When she told me what happened, I felt like it was confirmation from God that He heard my prayer and my cries. I went home that night and never worried about the situation again.

What does your salvation mean to you?

My salvation means everything to me. I know that Jesus died for my sins and I need to make sure that his death was not in vain. I try my best to abstain from committing sins, but I find comfort in knowing that if and when I do commit a sin, I am forgiven already.

If you could save someone by telling them one thing God has done for you in your life, what would it be?

God has spared my life in many ways. There are so many things that could have happened in my life due to the lifestyle I was living such as diseases, homelessness, incarceration, and the list goes on. I am disease free, never have been without a roof over my head, and never been incarcerated. Only by the grace of God was I spared, so I take every chance I get to tell someone to go to God and He will see you through.

Tell me why you couldn't imagine your life without God.

I couldn't imagine my life without God because I never want to feel what life was like without God. I never want to go back there. I know I learned many lessons living life without God, but I would have never recognized them as lessons had I not found God. I just can't imagine it; there is no life without God.

If you could describe your relationship with God, what would you say about it? How does it help you day to day?

PERFECT. It helps me to have comfort in knowing I am never alone in anything that I do.

****

According to *Webster's Dictionary*, promiscuous has many definitions, but I have selected three:

1. Having or involving many sexual partners
2. Including or involving too many people or things: not limited in a careful or proper way
3. Not restricted to one sexual partner

Let's focus on number three. Not restricted to one sexual partner; I find this the most interesting because it has the number one in it. Although these definitions talk about numerous partners, I heard at a women's conference that it didn't matter if you were with one individual and having sex with them, you were still being promiscuous because God intended sex for husbands and wives, not boyfriends or friends with benefits. Sex is sex, and if it isn't with your husband then it is wrong. In 1 Corinthians 7:9, it says, "…if they cannot exercise self-control, let them marry. For it is better to marry than to burn *with passion*."

****

God always places people in your life to be a vessel to bring you to Him. Many do not realize what God's voice sounds like. It can be in the form of another individual speaking to you confirming something you have been praying for; it can be something that you may have read, or something that you may have dreamt. He can speak to you through visions; He speaks to you by placing things in your heart and in your mind, but God will always speak to you through His Word. It takes time to build up your heart and mind to discern what is of God and what is not. But once you are mature, you will be able to speak with authority and results will come to pass because "faith comes by hearing, and hearing by the Word of God." (Romans 10:17 NKJV)

This young lady experienced a stranger telling her that "everything is going to be fine." That was definitely God! God placed that lady at the right place at the right time to confirm that "all is well."

Out From Darkness

Age: 28

Legal Assistant

> "In the time of my favor I will answer you,
> and in the day of salvation I will help you;
> I will keep you and will make you
> to be a covenant for the people,
> to restore the land
> and to reassign its desolate inheritances,
> [9] to say to the captives, 'Come out,'
> and to those in darkness, 'Be free!'"

Isaiah 49:8-9 NIV

Tell me what was your life like before Christ?

To tell you the truth, I always thought I was a Christian ever since I was brought up in a Catholic household living with my grandparents, moving from place to place all the time, and from country to country due to the nature of their work as diplomats. They taught me the values of what it meant to be a "Christian," but the thing is, I didn't receive my first bible until I was 15 years of age from my mom. For the longest while, I had been going to church like it was ritual, and yet, I never felt very connected to the Father (God). I would pray the "Hail Mary's" and the

"Our Father" prayers that were typical of the Catholic churchgoer, but I had no real relationship with the Lord.

When was it that I discovered that I had found the truth? My story begins after finding out at age 12 that my mother was raped when she was 15 by my father and had both me and my twin sister at the age of 16. She admitted that if she had had her way back in the day, she would have aborted us, but the only reason why she didn't have an abortion was because my grandparents didn't believe in abortion and believed that every child born belonged to God.

Even though I knew she was being real with me, the news shocked me and hurt me for a long, long time because I felt rejected. I felt so lost and didn't really know where my place was in the family after hearing the news. There were times I felt that my grandmother didn't like me until one day she said in the heat of the moment when we were having an argument that I looked just like my father (biological). I know that my grandmother said it in a fit of anger without thinking, to which I know she deeply regrets having said that and has long since apologized for saying it, however, the words still cut deeply into me, and although I had forgiven her for it, the truth was I began to despise who I was because of it. Words are so powerful that they are like arrows, once you shoot them, they never can return back until they've hit the target. I began to despise the rapist father that I had never met because I apparently looked like him. My identity was wrapped up in someone I had never known and had never met and was clearly hated by the whole family. I felt like an outsider even though I shouldn't have felt that way.

I landed in a place where I pretended to be happy, when in all truth; I struggled with suicidal tendencies and depression. I at one time sleepwalked into the kitchen at the age of 13, and found a large kitchen knife and drew it from the drawer, pointing it towards my chest while my grandmother was facing her back to me cooking something, not knowing I was in the room. For some reason, like as if someone tapped her on the shoulder, she turned around immediately as I was about to strike myself dead in a trance like state and ran towards me shouting at me to put the knife down. I responded and put the knife down and vaguely remember that I didn't really know how I got to the kitchen. Remember, I'm sleepwalking and have no control of my body, and yet, I was aware of my actions in a trance-like state that I was in. My grandmother was totally freaked out that I had sleep-walked into the kitchen with the intention of killing myself without really knowing what was going on. That was when I knew I had some spiritual issues I was dealing with. I experienced a lot of spiritual oppression for some years after that incident, which was one of many, that I knew that I was under some demonic attack. Despite these attacks, I still remained ignorant of God's saving grace and power, which is one of the reasons having received my bible at age 15 meant so much to me. I received so much insight, knowledge, healing, and deliverance when I discovered the Truth about Jesus, who was the One that set me free at a time that I needed spiritual shackles to be broken. I can declare with sincerity that Jesus is definitely the Way, the Truth, and the Life for me.

What drew you to Christ?

What drew me to Christ was when I received my first bible from my mother at the age of 15. It was the first time that I could read that book for myself and not wait until a Sunday service to wait for the priest (in Catholic church) to tell me about what it meant to be "Christian" through his own interpretation of the Bible. I wanted to know more about God for myself, and that is what the Word empowered me with. The knowledge of the Truth set me free from the ignorance I had lived with for many years that kept me in the dark struggling with demonic oppression and didn't seem to cease until I learned that in the name of Jesus, demons must flee, demons must bow, demons must declare that Jesus Christ is Lord. The power is in the name of Jesus, and once I accepted Him into my heart, my deliverance and healing from these oppressive spiritual experiences that I encountered for years all of a sudden ceased as I confessed my sins and the sins of my forefathers one by one, putting all of them under the blood.

What made you decide, the day you were saved, that that was the day to dedicate your life to God?

My mom, who was living in a different country at the time, had bought me a book by Dr. Rebecca Brown called *He Came to set the Captives Free*. This book was given to me after receiving my first bible from her. She, at that point, was "born again" and was telling me that it was time me and my sister consider what it means to be "born again." I still experienced demonic assaults as I was growing up, and when I read that book by Rebecca Brown, she talked about what it meant to be born again and gave me so much insight as to what curses were operating in my life. I was so drawn to the power of Christ that I decided to give my life to Christ. The funny thing was, when I made my decision to give my life away to Christ, my sister also agreed to give her life to Christ on the same day as me at the age of 15. When we said that prayer, I kid you not, there was a massive wind that rattled the living room we were in as we declared that Jesus Christ was our Lord and Savior. It was so violent and unexplainable because the windows were all shut at that time, and yet, the curtains were swishing about all over the place as if the windows had been open. To this day, we cannot explain how that could possibly happen, however, we started to have a lot more supernatural experiences after we gave our lives to the Lord, which would literally require me to write a book if I had to go in serious detail. But for the purpose of my testimony, what I will say is that after that day I gave my life to the Lord, I am convinced that there is no other way but Jesus.

What does your salvation mean to you?

My salvation brought to me much-needed spiritual deliverance from inherited curses that were operating in my life as a young child since the day I was born. It testifies that my salvation means I'm free through the power of Christ and by His blood. My sins could no longer keep me bound, nor could the sins of my forefathers keep me bound if I confessed them before the almighty God by seeking Him in all truth, and by choosing to no longer remain ignorant of the Truth that Jesus is the only way to the Father who is in Heaven. None can come to Him except through the Son, Jesus.

If you could save someone by telling them one thing God has done for you in your life, what would it be?

Although my earthly father failed me by not being there for my sister and my mother and me, God became my Father that day when my father abandoned us. There is a real love out there that does exist that is so powerful that it can break every chain of injustice that you've encountered in your life. I struggled with sleepwalking, depression, suicidal tendencies, and unexplainable spiritual attacks that would disable me, paralyze me, hurt me physically, and torment me emotionally. The moment I discovered the Truth, the Truth which is in Jesus, it literally set me free, and now I am free indeed. I no longer fear the powers of darkness that once used to invade half of my life. The answer that we need in discovering who we really are is all contained in the Bible. If you seek the Truth in all earnestness, you will find it if you look in the right place. For me, the Truth is in the Bible.

Tell me why you couldn't imagine your life without God.

When you've experienced the spiritual attacks I endured for many years, then discovered that there is a man called Jesus that can set you free, I feel like that woman with the issue of blood who endured that sickness for 12 long years and finally touched the hem of the garment of my Savior and discovered that this oppression is not my portion in life. I can be free and live freely indeed. I cannot go back to what life was like after encountering such liberation from such torment that invaded my life for years.

If you could describe your relationship with God, what would you say about it? How does it help you day to day?

My relationship with God is intimate. I hear Him more clearly than I ever did before. I've discovered that I have the gift of the prophetic working in my life, and many things I have spoken or dreamed have come to pass because I believe in the true and living and breathing Word of God. I feel like I'm still discovering new sides to the Father each day. I see myself as a little kid always asking for my Father's opinion on every little thing because, at the end of the day, it's not how the world sees you that counts, it is how your Heavenly Father sees you that does. That is how I communicate with Him each day, through prayer and meditation, works of service in my church, and continually increasing knowledge in His Word in order to remain in right standing. I am working at developing unshakable faith in Him because He is the Way, the Truth, and the Life. Without Him, life for me would be meaningless, and my freedom would not have come had I not decided that Jesus is the road to all Truth. I believe that I'm still learning to increase my faith and that I take each day as it goes. I discover the good, the bad, and the ugly about myself as the Lord removes all the things that are not like Him out of me so that I can become more like Him, made in His image and likeness because we were all created to be like God since the times of Genesis. He is my Alpha and Omega, and He is the rock on which I stand. People may come to ridicule my faith with their philosophies, but they cannot deny my own personal experience and encounters with God. My personal experience of Him makes me sure that He definitely does exist and I will stand by that Truth until my dying breath. I admit, I'm still a work in progress, but walking with God has been an amazing journey, and I still feel like I'm learning new sides of the Lord each day. It's a long-lasting, covenant relationship that I don't ever want to break, and that is how strong my relationship with the Lord is. I can't live without Him; I can't live without my Jesus, because He is Life itself.

****

This testimony reminds me of every scary movie that I saw as a little kid. Children often have fears of monsters being under the bed or in the closet. I truly believed that those monsters were demons trying to taunt children. For twenty years I never slept on my back. I gave too much credit the devil majority of my life because I was always in fear. I was waiting for Satan and his demons to attack me in my sleep. I can truly say that I lost hundreds, in fact thousands of hours of sleep over the years due to fear. It wasn't until someone prayed with me to have a peaceful night's rest that I started to sleep on my back to prove that I was putting my faith in God. This lasted for a few months, and the first night, I tossed and turned and woke up at least fifteen times making sure that I was not levitating in my sleep. After I had conquered that fear, I started having dreams that were of evil, and I always remember screaming Jesus' name or yelling Scripture at the devil to cast him away. I am surprised no one in my house heard me because I am pretty sure I was really screaming. In time, those evil dreams became a thing of the past and I asked Jesus for peace while I sleep because He is the Prince of Peace and I know He hears my prayers.

2 Timothy 1:7 says, "For God has not given us a spirit of fear, but of power and of love and of a sound mind." This scripture alone lets you know that this woman's testimony and my own fear were not of God but of the devil himself. We need to be well equipped with the Word of God to fight off these demons. When you are in the Word daily, and when you start to memorize key scriptures to bind any demon in the name of Jesus, you are exercising the authority that God has given you to "trample on serpents and scorpions and over all the power of the enemy, and nothing shall by any means hurt you" (Luke 10:19). But, be sure to no longer give place to Satan by talking about what he has done to you after you have bound him. Continue to stand on the Word of God and allow God to guide you with this problem.

Seek Wisdom in All That You Do

Age: 33

Centralized Access Coordinator

"⁵ Trust in the LORD with all your heart and lean not on your own understanding; ⁶ in all your ways submit to him, and he will make your paths straight."

Proverbs 3:5, 6 NIV

Tell me what was your life like before Christ?

My life before Christ was unfulfilled. I knew what I wanted for myself and for my son, which was to be married again and to have a second chance at having a family. Yet, I wasn't taking the necessary steps to find a mate that had God as the center of his life. I was in relationships that I knew were temporary, yet the comfort and pseudo love I got from these relationships helped me suppress my true emotions. Before Christ, I did not know how to love myself enough to feel as if I deserved more for myself.

What drew you to Christ?

My husband played a major role in my relationship with the Lord today. Being raised in a religion that made me feel as if everything I did was never good enough really drew me away from prayer and drawing close to God. Some of the decisions that were made for my life when I was younger were based on the beliefs of this religion and I grew angry because my mother did not know how to make her own decisions for me. Everything was based on what the "elders" said and not what was according to God's will. I am blessed to have a relationship today with God and have never felt closer to Him.

What made you decide, the day you were saved, that that was the day to dedicate your life to God?

I knew I was ready to dedicate my life to God on that day because I had finally forgiven myself for past sins. I was thinking and dwelling on the many mistakes I made in my previous marriage. I would talk to family and friends about my relationship, and regardless of my faults, they would only tell me what I wanted to hear and not what was necessary for me to save my marriage. I also thought about the fact that I wanted to have a child with my husband, but because I had abortions, I questioned if I would be able to have another child. I truly beat myself up for a long time based on all of the wrong I had done. I was finally able to let go and allow myself to be loved by God and forgive myself. I felt in my heart that He really loved me and wanted me to be in union with Him, and I was ready to embrace the second chance He has given me to get my life in order.

What does your salvation mean to you?

My salvation means that nothing in this world is more important than my relationship with God. I believe in His promise and in the ransom sacrifice of His son Jesus Christ and that one day I will have eternal life.

If you could save someone by telling them one thing God has done for you in your life, what would it be?

God answers prayers! It amazes me when I think of all He has done for me and my family. I asked God for very specific things to change in my life and He answered my prayers right on time. It's funny how sometimes I would pray to God and not even know what I really wanted, yet He knows and delivers in abundance. I asked God for a position at my job that would keep me in the same department, yet I also wanted to be a support for all of my clinics. The position that I got did not even exist! It was literally created just for me. I was the only person offered the position and I got it within a week. It is the schedule and flexibility that I wanted and it was a promotion. From the time I started praising God, He has answered all of my prayers.

Tell me why you couldn't imagine your life without God.

My life without God would be incomplete. I feel like everything I have and all that I want for my family in the future would never be enough without God's blessings and guidance. I cannot make any decisions without consulting with my Father in Heaven. If I don't get a response from Him, I will not do anything. The Bible says, "Do not lean on your own understanding but seek His guidance and wisdom in all we do."

If you could describe your relationship with God, what would you say about it? How does it help you day to day?

I would like to strengthen my relationship with God. I want to develop a strong prayer life, and at this point, I feel like I do not have that. When I am consistent in talking with God and praising Him daily, I feel whole. When I stay prayed up, I can make better decisions throughout the day and I feel more confident that He will guide my decisions.

****

Many of us as women can relate to this woman's testimony. How many of us have been in relationship after relationship after relationship, yearning for love that goes unfulfilled? We do not know why we do it, but we have a yearning desire to feel loved in all the wrong places.

For me, I grew up in a divided household—I had one parent who was married and the other single. I wanted the best of both worlds. I wanted to be in a loving relationship and I also wanted the perks of living the single life. Since the beginning of high school, I have been in relationships. Relationships that would last years and each one promised marriage and the world. Yet, I always wanted more. I truly believe that I grew up entirely too fast and wanted what most adults had. Today as an adult, I still want those things that the adults had, but I want them with God at the center. I want my future husband to search for me, but he will only find me once he is so deep in Christ; that is where we will meet. That is when I will say "I do" as this young lady has. She realized that her husband loved Christ and she knew that He too would be the center of her life because He was the center of her husband's life.

Your past has been forgiven once you accept Jesus Christ as your Lord and Savior. The Bible says, "Therefore, if anyone is in Christ, he is a new creation; old things have passed away; behold, all things have become new" (2 Corinthians 5:17 NKJV). Another verse says, "as far as the east is from the west, so far has he removed our transgressions from us" (Psalms 103:12 NIV). God has removed our sins from us; He removed any guilt, condemnation, or hurt from us, as this young lady mentions she "finally was able to let go and allow God to love her." That meant taking away any guilt from past sins she blamed herself for. She took another step toward the top of her mountain and dropped off a piece of baggage that was weighing her down.

When you seek God and ask Him for His wisdom, guidance, and love, He will bless you with more than you could ever imagine. Continue to pray, continue to read The Word, and continue to worship Him in the valleys. He will answer your prayers! Do not give up. Your breakthrough is just around the corner. "For [the Spirit which] you have now received [is] not a spirit of slavery to put you once more in bondage to fear, but you have received the Spirit of adoption [the Spirit producing sonship] in [the bliss of] which we cry, Abba (Father)! Father! The Spirit Himself [thus] testifies together with our own spirit, [assuring us] that we are children of God." (Romans 8:15, 16 AMP)

God's Everlasting Grace

Age: 28

Homemaker, Student, Certified Nurse's Assistant

"For by grace you have been saved through faith, and that not of yourselves; *it is* the gift of God, not of works, lest anyone should boast."

Ephesians 2: 8, 9

Tell me what was your life like before Christ?

For me, Christianity has always been a part of my life. I grew up in a Christian home, church on every Sunday in our Sunday's best. So it was just common in our family. I went to a Christian school and just followed the road for a while. I first gave my life to Christ in middle school, and you know, from then through high school I was involved in youth group, church retreats, etc. Once I got to college is when I went into the world so to speak; I didn't have the other believers that I had before. Also from a young age I struggled with homosexual tendencies that I still to this day struggle with. I found myself always Okaying the fact that I liked women. After a while I would not think about it. I would try to hide it, pray about it, and I finally realized that the feelings I felt were wrong. I have always wanted children and I realized that if I kept on with this lifestyle, I would not be able to fulfill that desire the way God intended it to be. Today I am grateful for the Christian influences I had in my life at such a young age.

Because of them, I am a proud wife and mother of two children.

What drew you to Christ?

I was always with Christ. I read my Bible, I went to church, but what really finally broke me to give all the things I struggle with to Him was when my husband and I split up and then we were working on getting back together. We started going to church together and started seeking counseling from our pastor, and that's when we were both broken. I am a firm believer that sometimes God has to break you down in all aspects for you to truly see that He is in control of it all. Believe me, I am not perfect. I struggle every day with the sins of my past, but I push through. God is my rock. I have to pray through it all and beg for forgiveness every moment of every day.

What made you decide, the day you were saved, that that was the day to dedicate your life to God?

About three months after my husband and I were in the church continuously, I finally broke down and gave it all to him. Giving it to God was the easy part, practicing every moment of every day was the hard part. I had to dive into the Word and get out of the world. There were times that I had to shut myself up and hide, but then I knew that doing that was not what God wanted. I had to be a pillar of strength to fight through my indiscretions and be a strong tower with my walk with God.

What does your salvation mean to you?

My salvation is so important. We cannot live without God; God is first and foremost, my Heavenly Father. I love Him first then my husband, then my children. Raising my children in the Word is the most important thing. I read with my son every morning Psalms and Proverbs. I do my own devotion afterwards, we pray every night before bed and every morning before school. I want my children to know and be in love with God just like I am.

If you could save someone by telling them one thing God has done for you in your life, what would it be?

I would tell them that God is a God of grace and mercy; He loves the sinner and will welcome you with open arms. God forgives the unforgiveable, that is what makes him God. He doesn't judge, he waits for you to come to Him, and over and over again He will wash you with His grace.

Tell me why you couldn't imagine your life without God.

I couldn't live without God because He knows all things. He has my life's path written in the palm of His hand and will not leave nor forsake me. Even if I backslide he's there to pick me up.

If you could describe your relationship with God, what would you say about it? How does it help you day to day?

God is my rock and my salvation. I can do all things through Him who strengthens me (Philippians 4:13). He helps me to push forward giving me the energy every day to get up and thank Him for another day and helping me to not worry about anything and give it to Him.

****

Homosexuality is something that many people suffer with today as this young lady does. Although she is free in Christ, she still struggles with it. We are human and the great part is that she has Christ on her side. She is a wife and a mother who cherishes the covenant that was made with God and her husband when they decided to marry. She will not act on these homosexual desires, but she continues to lean on God for strength. She knows that God will get her through this situation as He has helped her with other issues in her life.

There are many young children and adults struggling with their identities. Some of these young men and women are still in the adolescent stage and believe that they are interested in the same sex, or they want to be the opposite sex. It may be hard as mothers to relate and identify with this situation. You must be bold, you must stay in the Word, and you must stay on your knees praying for a healing. This is a spirit that is taking over the lives of many men and women of all ages. Remember, I mentioned in a previous chapter that you have the power and authority to cast away demons, but you must first accept Christ as your personal Lord and Savior.

This young lady realized that if she continued to give in to homosexual tendencies, she would not be able to become a mother naturally, which is something she always wanted to do. Today, many homosexual couples are able to adopt children. There is nothing wrong with wanting to be a parent to a child, however, the Bible says that "each man *should* have his own wife, and let each woman have her own husband" (1 Corinthians 7:2). Marriage is sacred and is between one man and one woman. In the Garden of Eden, God blessed Adam with Eve and told them to *be fruitful and multiply*. If these are strict instructions from God from the beginning, we must honor what our purpose is on this Earth.

Speak over your children and encourage them through the Word like this woman does. In due time, the spirit of homosexuality will flee in the name of Jesus. But, you must intercede first through prayer.

A Shift in the Atmosphere That Brought Inner Peace

Age: 27

Certified Medical Assistant / Ed Technician

"Come to me and I will give you rest—all of you who work so hard beneath a heavy yoke. Wear my yoke—for it fits perfectly—and let me teach you; for I am gentle and humble, and you shall find rest for your souls; for I give you only light burdens."

Matthew 11:28 TLB

Tell me what was your life like before Christ?

I was in a relationship for 10 years with a man that I thought I was going to marry, raise a family, and own a home with. We decided to take our relationship to the next step and move in together. I was very excited and slightly scared, but my excitement and love outweighed my fear (I should've realized that this fear was a sign to not go through with it). Looking back, there were red flags that I definitely should have paid more attention to, but my love overshadowed what I knew was right from wrong. Love is truly blind. I felt that he and I moving in together would help him mature as a man and nothing would be able to stop us.

As time went on, the maturity did not come. Financially it was a struggle because the person who I thought I went into this new adventure with completely checked out.

There was no WE; he was focused on himself and I was focused on getting us through financially and spiritually. I was digging myself in a hole financially and emotionally. My family and friends knew somewhat of what was going on but not the whole story. I was wearing a mask saying I'm OK on the outside but on the inside I was crying and heartbroken.

I continued to hang in there because my love for him was strong yet deep, and I prayed and hoped for change. As time went on, we were no longer on the same page. I was at the end of my rope and I wanted to know what our next step was going to be with our relationship. The conversation came and I was hit with a BOMB. I was told by the love of my life that two years ago he was unfaithful and possibly fathered a child. I was caught completely caught off guard. My heart was crushed! In my head I was driving myself crazy asking numerous questions. "Where do I go from here? What am I going to do? How will I pay for this apartment? What am I going to do?" He was the only one I had ever loved and known, but God's plan for my life removed him. With that, God has blessed me to maintain and keep my home. I now have peace within, I am constantly learning something new about myself, and I appreciate my alone time. The best is yet to come!! God answered my prayers and a change was made!

What drew you to Christ?

There is a specific moment I can recall that God was starting to draw me close to Him. During the time when I was living with my ex-boyfriend, there were many occasions where we were supposed to wake up and go to church, but we would oversleep or decide to sleep in. At some point, I started feeling the need to be in church more. This one particular Sunday, I woke up feeling that I needed to be in the presence of God. I said to my boyfriend, "Let's go to church" and his response was, "No." I lay in the bed for 10 minutes going back and forth, and his response was still "no." I remembered getting up and saying, "Well I'm going." His response wasn't "OK baby go to church and pray for us," it was "You are going to go without me." I responded "yes," and the strength I felt standing up for what I needed was amazing. Just knowing that I was pressing my way forward toward God on my own was great. I felt like it was a test from God saying, "Will you choose him or Me?" I chose God and I'm glad I did.

What made you decide, the day you were saved, that that was the day to dedicate your life to God?

I was baptized at an early age. I was following what my parents directed me to do, but as an adult dealing with life and different situations, in my heart Jesus was calling me and I answered His call by going to the altar and I joined my church.

What does your salvation mean to you?

My salvation is everything to me! It's my inner peace. It's what keeps joy in my heart and me smiling every day.

If you could save someone by telling them one thing God has done for you in your life, what would it be?

I could have easily gone down a road of depression or lost my mind when I went to through the breakup with my then boyfriend, but God saved me and kept my mind. He brought me out of a dark place. I would tell others that no matter what trust and believe in God. He knows what you are going through, just be still and know He is God.

Tell me why you couldn't imagine your life without God.

I couldn't imagine my life without God because without Him, I would have no vision, no peace, no guidance, and no purpose. I wouldn't be able to go through life situations without Him giving me the strength to press through.

If you could describe your relationship with God, what would you say about it? How does it help you day to day?

My relationship with God is one that is dear to my heart. When certain trials are thrown my way—my reaction is "Come on! Really?" There may be a month where money is extra tight, or I may go through an emotional battle, yet trying my best to sort them out. He works it out every time, I mean, every time. He has a way of getting a message to me that is needed for my spirit. It may be a message that I heard while in church, watching television, or just through conversation with others. It blows my mind, but that's just the power of God. I look back on how far he has brought me and just give thanks, and that encourages me to go hard for whatever He has planned for me.

****

A broken heart–that feeling you actually get when something as devastating as adultery hits your heart and you feel it break. How is it possible? The pain you feel in your heart and the feeling you get in your gut is indeed the worst feeling one can have. You can have it for many different reasons, but in this situation, it was the last thing she wanted to hear after 10 years of being in a relationship with someone she thought she had forever with.

I can remember having the rug pulled up from underneath me after riding on my cloud of love. The hurt I felt lasted months. I hated every single day of it. There is no greater hurt than to have something you loved lost forever. How does one learn to un-love? How do you move on every day? Where do you start to undo all of the patterns that you had set in stone for years? How do you find people to surround yourself with all over again? You cut all those friends off to put your man first. Where do you start?

You start with God. God has the answers to all of your problems. He has the answers to everything! You have the Bible, which can help you get through any issue at any time. What other book do you know of that can give you answers to today's issues 2000+ years after Jesus' death? The best thing about living in a technological world is having the internet at your fingertips through cell phones.

Look up your issue on your preferred search engine and type 'in the Bible' after it. You will pull up notable websites that will give you both devotionals and a list of scriptures relating to that issue.

Allow God to heal you. Allow God to be the love of your life. Allow Him to love you like no man, both male and female, can. Think of the love a parent may have for his/her child or children, now imagine greater than that. Imagine the love a husband and wife may have, and now imagine greater. You cannot physically imagine how vast God's love is for you. You can get an idea of how great His love is because He gave us His only begotten son to die for all of our sins. But, can you give up your son or daughter as a sacrifice? Most of us would say no. Allow God to wrap you in His arms. Allow Him to secure you in His love. Ask Him for help. Ask Him to show you His love in ways that you could never imagine. I am pretty sure you will experience what this young lady experienced. I am sure her heart was broken for a long time and it is possibly still broken, but God has continuously given her strength to move on from that relationship.

You are not going to get over this heartbreak in one day. Live each day, one day at a time. Do not look to the future. Do not feel that you will never find love. Lose yourself in God, and next thing you know, you are having coffee and dinner with some guy you met by accident who just so happens to go to your favorite restaurant all the time, who goes to your supermarket all the time, who lives in your development, who goes to your church! God will bring you your man. He brought Adam his woman, so tell me why this does not apply to you? Don't worry about it, but lose yourself in God. He will take care of the rest.

The Lord Saved Me

Age: 40

Retail Manager

"Wait *and* hope for *and* expect the Lord; be brave *and* of good courage and let your heart be stout *and* enduring. Yes, wait for *and* hope for *and* expect the Lord."

Psalms 27:14 AMP

Tell me what was your life like before Christ?

My life before Christ was hard, even as a baby. I was abused by my parents, my mom tried to sell me to a man when I was 13 for drugs. Since the age of 14, I've been in and out of foster care until I gave birth to my son at the age of 17. I was physically abused by men, exposed to drugs, and I witnessed my youngest son's father get murdered in front of me and my two children. Soon after, I was on drugs and I gave up my children because I didn't feel I deserved them. I hated myself. I was on drugs, partying all the time. I did everything that I could to stay numb to my reality. I was killing myself slowly until that day I almost died... God came and saved me.

What drew you to Christ?

I really don't remember because I was about nine when I started to attend church. However, my Dad had committed suicide when I was just a baby, and my mom was on drugs all of my childhood. I knew as a small child that no one but God would save me from the hurt, harm, and danger that lied ahead. Something in me knew I would not be able to make it without God—He was the way. I knew my life was going to be hard, and I knew I couldn't do it alone. That's what drew me to Christ; I needed protection.

What made you decide, the day you were saved, that that was the day to dedicate your life to God?

At the age of 19, my life took a turn for the worse. My youngest son's father was murdered in front of me and my two boys, and I started to take drugs (cocaine). I got very sick one day and almost died. As I lay in the hospital bed, the Holy Spirit came to save me by telling me to give my life to God and He will save you. A friend of mine took me to her house and reintroduced me to God at a church in Brooklyn, NY. I gave my life to God as an adult and I never did drugs again. When God saved my life, I knew by the time I got to the altar, I would dedicate my life to the Lord forever because He saved me. Faith without works is dead so you have to read the Word, mediate on it, and pray without ceasing!!! God can move mountains. I knew from the day I was saved that my life would never be the same and it is true, it hasn't been the same. My past is truly in the past.

What does your salvation mean to you?

Salvation to me means being saved from harm and also being delivered. Without God I would not be where I am today. My life is not perfect, I still struggle from time to time, but my Lord guides me, protects me, and covers both myself and my family in His blood. I've had so many life-and-death situations. Just a few years back, I was told I had cancer in my stomach. I prayed day-in and day-out along with my spiritual mother for healing and God healed me!!! He can do all things and I believe that!!! When the doctors ran the test again, there was no sign of any cancer! Just a few months ago they said my baby boy would have problems after birth. They said he may die soon as he is born because of the protein in my blood. My son is four months now and he is healthy!! Whatever man does God can un-do. I believe once you give your life to God, he will keep you. All you have to do is trust and believe in Him.

If you could save someone by telling them one thing God has done for you in your life, what would it be?

No matter how big the situation is, our Lord is bigger; our Lord gave his only begotten son for our sins for He loves the world. Trust and believe he will not let your foot slip; trust and believe in Him. Since I was a baby, my life had no happy moments. My only happiness was suicide. I hated my life with no mother, no father, living in and out of foster care my entire teenage years. I had my first son at 17, my second son at 19, and his father abused me and gave me drugs. My life was hell. I didn't even have an idea about how to be a mother because I never had one, but God! My savior, He kept me, He didn't judge me, He didn't talk behind my back; He protected me from every situation. I live my whole life on these scriptures:

Psalm 27:10-14
10 Though my father and mother forsake me,
the Lord will receive me.
11 Teach me your way, Lord;
lead me in a straight path
because of my oppressors.
12 Do not turn me over to the desire of my foes,
for false witnesses rise up against me,
spouting malicious accusations.
13 I remain confident of this:
I will see the goodness of the Lord
in the land of the living.
14 Wait for the Lord;
be strong and take heart
and wait for the Lord.

Tell me why you couldn't imagine your life without God.

I couldn't imagine my life without God because I had given up on life years ago. I had nothing to live for. I was lifeless and I was in so much pain. As soon as I gave my life to God, he blessed me with hope. I started reading His Word, the Bible. Psalms is my favorite! I read it when I'm down, and Proverbs strengthens me. I was blessed with the Holy Spirit, so I don't just do things without God's approval. In the case that I do, I often suffer the consequences and feel convicted. When I straddle the fence and try to do it without God, it becomes painful; but as soon as I get back right on the right path, He leads me in the right direction. God is my GPS, I am lost without Him.

If you could describe your relationship with God, what would you say about it? How does it help you day to day?

My relationship with God is like having a father I never had: He protects me, He teaches me, He shows me right and wrong, and sometimes He allows me get into situations so I can learn from them. He loves me despite my actions. I don't know where I would be without Him. I will praise him for the rest of days. Every situation, no matter what it is, I pray for the answer. I pray for guidance. I even thank him for any situation just the way it is, good or bad. It took me a long time but I trust Him with everything in me, that's how He helps me day to day.

****

Although this young lady dealt with death on many occasions, she managed to get through it. Death surrounded her from a young age—death of her spirit because of her father's suicide, physical deterioration, and also another form of death from her mother due to drug abuse. This resulted in abandonment. She witnessed the murder of her son's father, another form of death. Then she slowly started killing herself with alcohol and cocaine. Some would say that death was literally following her, but because God protects all of His children no matter who they are, He saved her from death. In a way, He resurrected her and brought her back to life. First Corinthians 5:17 states, "Therefore, if anyone *is* in Christ, *he is* a new creation; old things have passed away; behold, all things have become new." Amen!

This woman received the best Daddy in the world! She was adopted into the family of God (Romans 8:15). Made a king in the Kingdom of God, she can now eat at the King's table and can benefit from all of the riches and glory by Christ Jesus. She now has the gift of grace. "For by grace you have been saved through faith, and that not of yourselves; *it is* the gift of God, not of works, lest anyone should boast" (Ephesians 2:8-9). She now has unlimited access to the Healer who was able to heal her of cancer, and He healed her newborn son. Only God can do all of these things. Only God can allow you to feel alive and renewed. Only God adopts you and allows you to call Him, Abba! Father! (Galatians 4:6). That is true love. All the glory and honor belongs to Him!

Loved, Forgiven, and Healed by God

To

Love, Forgive, and Heal Others in Jesus Name!

Age: 43

Behavior Trainer Assistant

"Be kind and compassionate to one another, forgiving each other, just as in Christ God forgave you."

Ephesians 4:32 NIV

Tell me what was your life like before Christ?

I was born at a time when my parents were ministers in a church my father pastored. Their relationship ended in separation and that left me with vague memories of momentary and limited visits of my father on a couple of Christmas mornings where my mother was often not present due to their broken relationship. I rarely attended church as a young child but remember attending the church across the street from my house for a summer meal event they had. We needed to attend service and then receive a bag full of delicious lunch items. There is a song I remember learning from that service and it has always been imbedded in my spirit. It is called, "It's

Bubbling." Basically, the song is a fun way of expressing how it feels to have Jesus in our soul.

The next part of my life was the bulk of my childhood experience with church-going. It was when I was left to live with my elderly grandparents. This was my real Pentecostal experience. The long skirts, the veil covering my head, the limited time with friends and family due to church attendance, and the dreadful message of "Jesus is coming, Jesus is coming!" As an adult, I have come to appreciate that early church experience because I love me some church. I can go every day that there is a service, but my mature Christian side has taught me to have balance. Before I met Christ, I worked in a Pediatric Dental office in Brooklyn, NY. It was a much-needed job I had acquired during my last year of high school. As a teen wife and teen mother of a wonderful little girl, I found myself far from the ways of the Lord. But He met me one day at my workplace. One day, my coworker asked me if I knew Jesus. I told her that I attended church when I was a little girl. I attended a youth program every Thursday and mentioned my dad was a pastor. Then she asked me again, "Do you know Jesus?" The thing was that my husband and I had just separated that very week and I needed to know Jesus for myself. I didn't make a public confession of Christ as my personal Lord and Savior that day at my job, but she invited me to a special Christmas service that both my husband and I both attended and where my journey of faith began.

What drew you to Christ?

Immediately after that Christmas service, I realized that I needed to make a decision for Christ on my own and not depend on the fact that my ancestors and family members were believers or ministers. I was given an English King James Version of the Holy Bible and was told by my co-worker who asked me, "Do you know Jesus?" that I should begin reading the Gospel of John. Although I was the valedictorian of all my graduating classes at this point, I never was an avid reader. I read because I needed to read, but never read for enjoyment. But when I began reading the Gospel of John, I found that those pages came to life for me. I read every morning on the 45-minute bus ride to and 45-minute bus ride from work. I began reading right before I went to bed, and one day, as I lie down on my bed reading the Word, I fell asleep with the Bible in hand. That night I had a dream. I dreamt that I was in a Christian book store and there were other believers there who were looking to purchase Christian paraphernalia. As I stood in front of a book stand, the Holy Spirit showed me a man in the store who was looking to see who knew the scriptures or not. He recited scripture better than many Christians I had known at that time. I woke up with the revelation that as Christians, we need to be armed with the Word of God because Satan knows the scriptures too, and He will use them to his advantage. All revelation and prophesy must align to God's Word and God's Word must be the ruler by which we measure every "Word" spoken to us as..."Thus saith the Lord." My love for the Word of God helped me to see life in a whole new perspective. I learned Jesus' way. I learned that He loves me. I received that love and acquired faith to put my whole life in His hands. The way Jesus did miracles, the way he interacted with the religious folk and the sinner truly impacted my relationship with others and immediately those around me noticed a difference in my life.

My prayer life was brought to a level of more than just asking for things, it turned into a time of fellowship with the Lord, a time to go deeper in my relationship with Him. I asked for more than earthly possessions, I asked that He would save, heal, and deliver my family members, young and old. I prayed for more than my needs, but focused on what He needed of me. I also got to know Christ more as I prayed His Word. He would reveal His purpose and plan for my life, and here I am, sharing what He has done thus far.

What made you decide, the day you were saved, that that was the day to dedicate your life to God?

My wonderful mother, may she rest in peace, for as long I can remember was a single mother. Therefore, I had limited contact with my biological father. After I got married, my husband and I moved into our first apartment in the Bushwick section of Brooklyn, and it so happens that my father graduated seminary not too far from where I lived and then opened a church three blocks from my home. One of my older sisters was a founding member of this church, and one day, she invited me to attend the service. I never shared what I was going through with anyone because of fear of what my family would do, but one of my older sisters knew and only she knew, and she invited me to a service one Sunday afternoon. The preacher at my father's church was preaching that afternoon and I envisioned my husband in a terrible state of health as the message was being delivered and the preacher kept talking about my situation and I couldn't speak, but all I could do was weep. I was at the altar, not the floor level, but the actual altar and embraced my father who was interceding there. I didn't do much of anything but put my arms around him and fell straight down to my knees and gave my life to God.

What does your salvation mean to you?

I treasure my salvation. I know that I have done nothing to deserve it, and could never do anything to keep it, but only keep my faith in Christ. I understand that I was bought at a price and it took the shedding of the blood of the innocent Lamb of God to save me, to rescue me from the grips of sin that I was bound to: unforgiveness, bitterness, anger, strife, and from the pain that the enemy imposed on me so that I don't live the abundant life that Jesus paid for through His death. The Bible says that "the devil came to steal, kill and destroy, but Jesus came that we may have life and that we might have it more abundantly," (John 10:10). I love my life now, and the life I now live in Christ.

If you could save someone by telling them one thing God has done for you in your life, what would it be?

God has shown me how to love others through extending forgiveness. If you are hurting and the pain is unbearable, you can't think, talk about, or look at the person who has hurt you. I want you to take a look at Christ on the Cross. He was bruised for our transgressions; His hands were pierced for our sins; His head bashed in, and forehead crowned with thorns. You think that the lashing out of others is painful. Think about the 39 lashes Jesus received on His back with not just words that hurt but with a whip that had metal pieces wrapped around the strings at the end of that whip. Imagine a sword piercing His side, nails piecing his feet to hold him up to take the pain and suffering you are now experiencing. If anyone can identify with pain and suffering, it's Jesus. When I saw the pain the bloodshed, the horrific death of my Lord and Savior Jesus Christ, I noticed that my pain didn't compare to His sacrifice for the forgiveness of my sin. Why couldn't I just put my pain on Him once and for all? He took that pain already for me; I just needed to recognize that He took it so I didn't have to hold that pain any more. Jesus suffered for the forgiveness of our sins because He loves us. In the same manner, as a follower of Christ, let it go. Give that pain to Jesus. Did you ever think that your suffering may have come as a result of your sin? The Bible says for "All have sinned and fall short of the Glory of God." Tell Him that you understand that and that you accept His forgiveness. He died on the cross for you. Accept His forgiveness, and as a result, offer forgiveness to those who made you suffer.

Tell me why you couldn't imagine your life without God.

I was reunited with my best friend from high school last year, and the first thing she told me was that she was worried that she would never find me. She thought I would be dead. She didn't want to imagine that but she could only come to that conclusion due to the way my husband treated me in my early years of marriage. As I reflect on all I have gone through as a young married, teen mother, I can truly say that if the Lord had not come to my rescue, I would've been in a mental institution, incarcerated, or worse, dead. I know that the day the Lord touched me He gave me hope for a better future. My life changed. He was my Lord now. He had my life in His hands. He protected me now. My family is numerous, but they couldn't do for me what the Lord has done for me. He has healed my brokenness. He has given me a hope.

If you could describe your relationship with God, what would you say about it? How does it help you day to day?

God is my Heavenly Father. Through the gift of His Holy Spirit I can call Him "Abba Father," which is a way of calling on God as my personal father, my daddy—the father who cares for me and who is not absent from my life. A daddy who wants to see a smile on my face. One who tells me don't cry, and who heals my wounds using His anointed servants to give me that right-now Word—that uplifting prayer or that whisper in my spirit-man to make me stronger so that I can get through my internal struggles, my family problems, future endeavors, meet my goals, celebrate my accomplishments, and to move me forward as He ushers me into my call and my purpose so that I operate in my destiny and my life-encouraging work. A providing Father that meets every single one of my emotional, physical, material, and spiritual needs. He is my friend when my friends are not around. I can tell Him anything and everything. As I walk and relate with Him every day, He uses my life experiences to counsel others and to encourage others to put their trust in the Lord. God has been so reliable, faithful, truthful, and He has never ever let me down so I trust Him for everything and with everything.

****

Joy Comes in the Morning

Age: 51

Retail Bank Manager / Mom

"For I am convinced that neither death nor life, neither angels nor demons, neither the present nor the future, nor any powers, neither height nor depth, nor anything else in all creation, will be able to separate us from the love of God that is in Christ Jesus our Lord."

Romans 8:38, 39 NIV

Tell me what was your life like before Christ?

My life was not fulfilled. I always felt like I was missing something to complete who I was or who I was meant to be. It was something I had always felt, but that sense of missing was there.

What drew you to Christ?

Well, I was raised to be a strong Catholic by a very strong and spiritual mother who I lost early in my life and, along with my dad, both had died so young. Having been through that and a marriage that was failing, I had to really search for what I always knew of…GOD.

People speak of this beautiful man who died for our sins and rose from the dead and who promises eternal life…I needed to know more. My mom always spoke of her commitment to God and the unity of the family. I guess I may have mistaken what my mom was speaking of being young and all, but I tried to keep my family together through a lot of terrible times. I almost lost my daughter to suicide because of the pain we were all going through. I decided that I needed to make a decision, and that was to get my family back on track. I needed to understand the Word of God and I need to find the love and happiness within my own heart. I needed to learn about this silence that I knew nothing of. I wanted to be able to hear the words being spoken to me. I always loved God because that was what I was taught as a child, but now I understand why I love my God. He comforts me…He guides me….He strengthens me and I feel all of it.

While I was getting my family back on track, I filed for divorce and I needed to…I know that it is frowned upon in my religion, however, I truly believe my God forgives me and knows the decision I made was in the best interest of my beautiful children and myself. There was no seeking any help for a person who had spiraled out of control, so I needed to make a decision, and the best decision for my children and me. Some people may not understand, but I live for God, my children, and myself. I cannot worry about what other people think. I needed to move forward for the people I love the most and my three cats.

What made you decide, the day you were saved, that that was the day to dedicate your life to God?

I think of this often…LENT….I always have such a hard time giving up something I love to eat and I know that sounds so two-faced, however, I made a decision that since food is so hard to give up and I don't use foul language, that I need to **give** more. I decided that I would start praying the rosary every day. I went from once a day to twice a day, and during lent, I always give my time towards prayer. There are days that I pray up to six times a day, and those are the days I love. I find comfort in prayer and I find comfort within His presence. When I say His presence I mean I feel His embrace around me, holding me, comforting me, guiding me, and those who know me know that He must spend quite a bit of overtime on me, and I feel His love.

What does your salvation mean to you?

My salvation is something I work towards every day. I feel like I get closer towards salvation with prayer.

If you could save someone by telling them one thing God has done for you in your life, what would it be?

Never give up…God has a plan for everyone!!! However, you need to make room for God in your life. I personally keep Him front and center because He is my salvation. I truly believe that if more people took the time to share their love of God that they could see past certain situations and not overreact. Learn to move on with love.

Tell me why you couldn't imagine your life without God.

I would feel empty–complete emptiness. There is no love without the love of God....He started it. Like I said before, I always knew of Him but I need to know him on a different level...my level.

If you could describe your relationship with God, what would you say about it? How does it help you day to day?

My relationship with God is one of the longest relationships I have ever had. I love Him and He loves me. I feel his presence constantly and I laugh when I see or hear something that says WWJD (What Would Jesus Do?) and I always imagine "I GOT THIS" in a *Madea* voice (she laughs).

I truly believe that keeping God front and center every day, in my thoughts, in prayers, and in my actions, tells me who I am. I define myself by keeping this relationship strong. I thank Him every day for the great giving's He has given me, and that I share with everyone.

I am not a rich person and actually, I walked away from a marriage with my beautiful children and that's all I needed to take the first steps towards the future. Without God's strength around me, I don't know if I would have come this far. All I know is that I love Him and He protects me and my children every day. My love for Him will never fade away. This is an eternal love.

****

I remember first reading this testimony and thinking wow, you would never be able to tell that this woman comes from a different denomination than I do because we believe in a lot of the same things.

She believes in Jesus, she believes in the love of Jesus, she sees the importance of prayer, she too would feel lost if she didn't have Him, and she wants to know what God's voice sounds like. However, when I pray I just lift my hands, or I lift my head, or I drop to my knees and pray to God. I do not use the rosary, I do not pray to saints, nor do I go to mass. I love that Christ is known in many religions around the world. I love that Jesus will help anyone, but I want to give her everlasting life. I don't want her to be tied down to the rules of religion such as what she mentioned with Lent. I want her to have complete freedom. I want you to have complete freedom. I want you to no longer feel bound to your marriage because your religion says that you cannot divorce. God does not want you to be in an unhealthy marriage. This woman knew it was time to remove herself from a failing marriage.

Some of you may feel obligated to stay in your relationships, but you do not have to. "God shall supply all of your needs." Take that step and do what is right for you or for your family. If you are bound to your job, if you are currently unemployed and praying for a job, if you are experiencing sickness in your life, if the doctor has given you a negative report and says you have a few months to live, allow God to come into your life and heal you. Allow God to come into your life and take over! If you are experiencing heartbreak, if you are struggling with homosexual tendencies, if you are an orphan, drug addict, adulterer, murderer, thief, or you are living in the past and cannot move forward. Right now is the time to say this prayer out loud and accept Jesus Christ into your life. Matthew 10:32 says, "Therefore whoever confesses Me before men, him I will also confess before My Father who is in heaven." Repeat this prayer:

Heavenly Father,

Thank you for this day of life,

Thank you for loving me so much that you sent your son,

Jesus Christ, to die on the cross for my sin.

I believe in my heart that Jesus Christ is the son of God and

On the third day he rose again.

Today I ask that you come into my life to become my Lord and Savior.

I am born again, I am saved, and I am a new creation.

My best days are ahead of me. Thank you Lord.

I love you, in Jesus' name. Amen.

Welcome to the Kingdom of God!

"For God so loved the world that He gave His only begotten Son, that whoever believes in Him should not perish but have everlasting life."

Please find a bible based church and allow God to perform miracles in your life. You will not regret it. These women are living proof of what God is doing and what He has done.

Thank you for reading and pass this book on to a friend so you can be a blessing in their life.

"That is, that we may be mutually strengthened *and* encouraged *and* comforted by each other's faith, both yours and mine."

Romans 1:12 AMP

God bless you.

Coming Spring 2014

The Past is in the Past so let it Pass:

For Men

By: Nadia Atkinson

www.ingramcontent.com/pod-product-compliance
Lightning Source LLC
Chambersburg PA
CBHW071518040426
42444CB00008B/1699